ADVICE FOR SEEKERS

CRCFELLOWSHIP
BURNABY
604 527 7200

D1012743

ADVICE FOR SEEKERS

*

C. H. SPURGEON

THE BANNER OF TRUTH TRUST

THE BANNER OF TRUTH TRUST
3 Murrayfield Road, Edinburgh EH12 6EL
PO Box 621, Carlisle, Pennsylvania 17013, USA

★

© The Banner of Truth Trust 1993
First Banner of Truth edition 1993
Reprinted 1999
ISBN 0 85151 651 3

★

Printed and bound in Great Britain by
Caledonian International Book Manufacturing Ltd,
Glasgow

Contents

1

Do Not Try to Save Yourself

If you think about it, God's value of heaven and yours are very different things. His salvation, when he set a price upon it, was to be brought to men only through the death of his Son. But you think that your good works can win the heaven which Jesus Christ, the Son of God, procured at the cost of his own blood! Do you dare to put your miserable life in comparison with the life of God's obedient Son, who gave himself even to death? Does it not strike you that you are insulting God? If there is a way to heaven by works, why did he put his dear Son to all that pain and grief? Why the scenes of Gethsemane? Why the tragedy on Golgotha, when the thing could be done so easily another way? You insult the wisdom of God and the love of God.

There is no attribute of God which self-righteousness does not impugn. It debases the eternal perfections which the blessed Saviour magnified, in order to exalt the pretensions of the creature which the Almighty spurns as vain and worthless. The trader may barter his gold for your trinkets and glass beads, but if you give all that you have to God it would be utterly rejected. He will bestow the milk and the honey of his mercy without money and without price, but if you come to him trying to bargain for it, it is all over for you; God will not give you choice provisions of his love that you do not know how to appreciate.

The great things you propose to do, these works of yours, what comparison do they bear to the blessing which you hope to obtain? I suppose by these works you hope to obtain the favour of God and procure a place in heaven. What is it, then, you propose to offer? What could you bring to God? Would you bring him rivers of oil, or the fat of ten thousand animals? Count up all the treasures that lie beneath the surface of the earth; if you brought them all, what would they be to God? If you could pile up all the gold reaching from the depths of the earth to the highest heavens, what would it be to him? How could all this enrich his coffers or buy your salvation? Can he be affected by anything you do to augment the sum of his happiness, or to increase the glory of his kingdom? If he were hungry he would not tell you. 'The cattle upon ten thousand hills are mine', he says (*Ps.* 50:10). Your goodness may please your fellow-creatures, and your charity may make them grateful, but will God owe anything to you for your gifts, or be in debt to you for your influence? Absurd questions! When you have done everything, what will you be but a poor, unworthy, unprofitable servant? You will not have done what you ought, much less will there be any balance in your favour to make atonement for sin, or to purchase for you an inheritance in the realms of light.

You who are going to save yourselves by reforms, and by earnest attempts and endeavours, let me ask you, if a man could not perform a certain work when his arm had strength in it, how will he be able to perform it when the bone is broken? When you were young and inexperienced, you had not yet fallen into evil habits and customs. Though there was depravity in your nature then, you had not become bound in the iron net of habit, yet even then you went astray like a lost sheep and you followed after evil. What reason have you to suppose that you can suddenly change the bias of your heart, the course of your actions and the tenor of your life, and become a new man? 'Can the Ethiopian change his skin, or the leopard his spots?' (*Jer.* 13:23). Are there not ten thousand probabilities against one that as you sinned before you will sin still? You found the pathway of evil to be so attractive and fascinating that you were enticed into it, and you will still be enticed and drawn away from that path of integrity which you are now so firmly resolved to tread.

The way to heaven by following the law given at Mount Sinai is very steep and narrow, and it takes only one wrong step for a man to be dashed to pieces. Stand at the foot and look up at it if you dare. On its brow of stone there is the black cloud, out of which lightning leaps and the blast of the trumpet sounds loud and long. Do you not see Moses tremble, and will you dare to stand unabashed where Moses is fearful and afraid? Look upwards, and give up the thought of climbing those steep crags, for no one has ever striven to clamber up there in the hope of salvation without finding destruction among the terrors of the way! Be wise, give up that deceitful hope of salvation which your pride leads you to choose and your presumption would soon cause you to rue.

Suppose you could do some great thing, which I am sure you cannot, and it were possible that you could from now on be perfect, and never sin again in thought, or word, or deed; how would you be able to atone for your past delinquencies? Shall I call for a resurrection in that graveyard of your memory? Let your sins rise up for a moment, and pass in review before you. Ah, the sins of your youth may well frighten you; those midnight sins; those midday sins; those sins against light and knowledge; those sins of body; those sins of soul! You have forgotten them, you say, but God has not. Look at the file! They are all placed there, all registered in God's daybook, not one forgotten—all to be read against you in the day of the last judgment.

How can future obedience make up for past transgression? The cliff has fallen and though the wave washes up ten thousand times, it cannot set the cliff up again. The day is bright but still there was a night, and the brightest day does not obliterate the fact that once it was dark. The self-righteous

[3]

man knows that what he is doing cannot satisfy God, for it cannot satisfy himself; and though he may perhaps drug his conscience, there is generally enough left of the divine element within the man to make him feel and know that it is not satisfactory.

To believe what God says, to do what God commands, to take that salvation which God provides—this is man's highest and best wisdom. Open your Bible. It is the pilgrim's guide, in which God describes the glory yet to be revealed. This is the one message of the gospel, 'Believe and live.' Trust in the incarnate Saviour, whom God appointed to stand in the place of sinners. Trust in him and you shall be saved.

2

Despised Ones Seeking Jesus

'Then all the tax collectors and the sinners drew near to Him to hear Him.' Luke 15:1

The most depraved and despised classes of society formed an inner ring of hearers around our Lord. I gather from this that he was a most approachable person, that he welcomed human confidence and was willing that men should commune with him.

Eastern monarchs affected great seclusion, and were likely to surround themselves with impassable barriers of state. It was very difficult for even their most loyal subjects to approach them. You remember the case of Esther, who, even though the monarch was her husband, still risked her life when she presented herself before King Ahasuerus, for there was a commandment that no one should come before the king unless they were called, at peril of their lives. It is not so with the King of kings. His court is far more splendid; his person is far more worshipful; but you may draw near to him at all times without hindrance. He has set no men-at-arms around his palace gate. The door of his house of mercy is wide open. Over the lintel of his palace gate is written, 'For every one that asketh receiveth; and he that seeketh findeth; and to him that knocketh it shall be opened' (*Matt.* 7:7).

Even in our own day great men are not easily approached. There are so many back stairs to be climbed before you can reach the official who might help you, so many servants to be passed by, that it is very difficult to achieve your objective.

The good men may be affable enough themselves, but they remind us of the old Russian fable of the hospitable house-holder in a village who was willing to help all the poor who came to his door, but who kept so many big dogs loose in his yard that nobody was able to get to the threshold, and there-fore his personal affability was of no use to anyone. It is not so with our Master.

Though the Lord Jesus Christ is greater than the greatest, and higher than the highest, he has been pleased to put out of the way everything which might keep the sinner from enter-ing into his halls of gracious entertainment. From his lips we hear no threats against intrusion, but hundreds of invitations to enter into the dearest intimacy. Jesus is to be approached not every now and then, but at all times, and not by some favoured few, but by all in whose hearts his Holy Spirit has kindled the desire to enter into his secret presence.

The philosophical teachers of our Lord's day affected very great seclusion. They considered their teachings to be so pro-found that they were not to be uttered in the hearing of the common multitude. 'Far hence, ye profane', was their scorn-ful motto. They stood on a lofty pillar of their fancied self-conceit and occasionally dropped down a stray thought upon the common herd beneath, but they did not condescend to talk familiarly with them, considering it a dishonour to their philosophy to communicate it to the multitude. One of the greatest philosophers wrote over his door, 'Let no one who is ignorant of geometry enter here'. But our Lord, compared with whom all wise men are fools—who is, in fact, the wis-dom of God—never drove away a sinner because of his ignor-ance, never refused a seeker because he was not yet initiated and had not taken the previous steps in the ladder of learn-ing, and never permitted any thirsty spirit to be chased away from the crystal spring of divine truth. His every word was a diamond, and his lips dropped pearls, but he was never more at home than when speaking to the common people, and teaching them about the kingdom of God.

Our Lord Jesus is said to be the *Mediator* between God and man. The office of mediator implies at once that he should be approachable. A mediator is not a mediator for one side—he must be close to both the parties between whom he mediates. If Jesus Christ is to be a perfect mediator between God and man, he must be able to come so near to God that God shall call him his fellow, and then he must approach man so closely that he shall not be ashamed to call him brother. This is precisely the case with our Lord.

Think about this, you who are afraid of Jesus. He is a mediator, and as a mediator you may come to him. Jacob's ladder reached from earth to heaven, but if he had cut away half a dozen of the bottom rungs, what use would the ladder have been? Who could climb up it to the hill of the Lord? Jesus Christ is the great conjunction between earth and heaven, but if he will not touch the poor mortal man who comes to him, then of what use is he to the sons of men? You do need a mediator between your soul and God; you must not think of coming to God without a mediator; but you do not want any mediator between yourselves and Christ. There is a necessary qualification for coming to God—you must not come to God without a perfect righteousness; but you may come to Jesus without any qualification, and without any righteousness, because as Mediator he has in himself all the righteousness and fitness that you require, and is ready to bestow them upon you. You may come boldly to him right now; he waits to reconcile you to God by his blood.

Another of Christ's offices is that of *Priest*. That word 'priest' has come to smell very badly nowadays; but it is a very sweet word as we find it in Holy Scripture. The word 'priest' does not mean a gaudily-dressed pretender, who stands apart from other worshippers, two steps higher than the rest of the people, and professes to have power to dispense pardon for human sin. The true priest was truly the

[7]

brother of all the people. There was no man in the whole camp of Israel so brotherly as Aaron. In fact, Aaron and the priests who succeeded him were so much the first points of contact with men, on God's behalf, that when a leper became too unclean for anybody else to approach, the last man who touched him was the priest. The house might be leprous, but the priest went into it; the man might be leprous, but he talked with him and examined him; and if afterwards that diseased man was cured, the first person who touched him must be a priest. 'Go, show thyself to the priest,' was the command to every recovering leper; and until the priest had entered into fellowship with him, and had given him a certificate of health, he could not be received into the Jewish camp.

The priest was the true brother of the people, chosen from among themselves, at all times to be approached; living in their midst, in the very centre of the camp, ready to make intercession for the sinful and the sorrowful. Surely, you will never doubt that if Jesus perfectly sustains the office of priest, as he certainly does, he must be the most approachable of beings: approachable by the poor sinner, who has given himself up to despair, whom only a sacrifice can save; approachable by the foul harlot who is put outside the camp, whom only the blood can cleanse; approachable by the miserable thief who has to suffer the punishment of his crimes, whom only the great High Priest can absolve. No other man may care to touch you, O trembling outcast, but Jesus will. You may be separated from all of humankind, justly and righteously, by your iniquities, but you are not separated from that great Friend of sinners who at this very time is willing that publicans and sinners should draw near to him.

As a third office, let me mention that the Lord Jesus is our *Saviour*; but I do not see how he can be a Saviour unless he can be approached by those who need to be saved. The priest and the Levite passed by on the other side when the bleeding man lay on the road to Jericho; they were not saviours,

[8]

therefore, and could not be, but he was the saviour who came where the man was, stooped over him, and took wine and oil and poured them into the gaping fissures of his wounds, and lifted him up with tender love and set him on his own beast, and led him to the inn. He was the true saviour; and, O sinner, Jesus Christ will come just where you are, and your wounds of sin, even though they are putrid, will not drive him away from you. His love shall overcome the nauseating offensiveness of your iniquity, for he is able and willing to save those who are like you. I might mention many other offices of Christ, but these three are sufficient. Certainly if the Spirit blesses them, you will be led to see that Jesus is not hard to reach.

3

Seekers Touching Christ

Some of us have ourselves been healed, and therefore speak from assured experience. One man I know was secretly bowed down with despondency and depression of an unusual sort—his life had been spent at the very gates of hell because of a great sorrow of heart when he was a youth; yet, in a moment, he was lifted into perfect peace by simply looking to him who was crucified upon the cross. That one form of healing is typical of others; for all other evils are overcome in the same manner. Jesus can heal you of your pride; he can deliver you from anger; he can cure you of sluggishness; he can purge you from envy, from lasciviousness, from malice, from gluttony, from every form of spiritual malady. And this he can do, not by the torturing processes of penance, or the exhausting labours of superstitious performance, or the fiery ordeals of suffering; but the method is simply a word from him, and a look from you, and all is done. You have only to trust in Jesus and you are saved; made a new creature in an instant; set on your feet again to start a new life with a new power within you which shall conquer sin. We who bear this testimony claim to be believed. We are not liars. Not even for God's honour would we palm a pious fraud upon you. We have felt in ourselves the healing power of Christ. We have seen it, and see it every day, in the cases of others, in persons of all ranks, and of all ages. All who have obeyed the word of Jesus have been made new creatures by his power. It is not one or two of us who bear this witness; there are hundreds of thousands who certify to the self-same fact; and not ministers alone, but other professions and callings. There are tradesmen, there are gentlemen, there are working men, there are persons high and low, who could say, 'We too are witnesses that Christ can heal the soul.' *I am too.*

Here, then, is the marvel—that those who know this do not immediately throng to Christ to obtain the self-same blessing. The behaviour of those of whom we read in the Gospels was a rational one. They heard that Christ had healed many, and their practical logic was, 'Let us be healed too!' Where is he? Let us reach him. Are there crowds about him? Let us jostle one another, let us force our way into the mass until we touch him, and feel the healing virtue flowing from him. But now men seem to have taken leave of their reason. They know that the blessing is available, an eternal blessing not to be weighed with gold, nor compared with diamonds; and yet they turn their backs upon it! Selfishness usually attracts men to places where good things are to be gained; but here is the best thing of all—the possession of a sound soul, the gaining of a new nature which will enable a man to share eternal glory with angels of light—which is freely available, yet man, being untrue to himself, does not even let a right-minded selfishness govern him, turns away from the fountain of all goodness and goes into the wilderness to perish of eternal thirst.

The gospel is preached to you, and God has not sent it with the intention that after you have heard it you should seek mercy and not find it. God does not tantalize, he does not mock the sons of men. He asks you to come to him. Repent and believe, and you shall be saved. If you come with a broken heart, trusting in Christ, there is no possibility that he will reject you; otherwise he would not have sent the gospel to you. There is nothing that so delights Jesus Christ as to save sinners. We never find that Jesus was in a huff because the people pressed about him to touch him. No, it gave him divine pleasure to give out his healing power. You who are in a trade are never happier than when business is brisk; and my Lord Jesus, who follows the trade of soul-winning, is never happier than when his great business is moving on rapidly. What pleasure it gives a physician when at last he brings a person through a severe illness into health! I think the medical profession must be one of the happiest engagements in the world when a man is skilful in it. Our Lord Jesus feels a most divine pleasure as he bends over a broken heart and binds it up. It is the very heaven of Christ's soul to be doing good to the sons of men. You misjudge him if you think he wants to be argued with and persuaded to have mercy; he gives it as freely as the sun pours out light, as the heavens drop with dew and as clouds yield their rain. It is his honour to bless sinners; it makes him a name, and an everlasting sign that shall never be removed.

I know that I, too, once belied him; when I felt my sins to be a great burden I said within myself, 'I will go to Jesus, but perhaps he will reject me.' I thought I had much to feel and to do to make myself ready for him, and I therefore did this and that, but the more I did the worse I became. I was like the woman who spent her money on physicians and did not get better, but rather grew worse. I fully understood that there was life in a look at Christ, that all I needed to do was simply to trust, to come as I was and put my case into his dear pierced hands, and leave it there, yet I still did not think it could be so; it seemed so simple—how could it be true? Was that all? I thought when I came to him he would say to me, 'Sinner, you have rejected me so long, you have mocked me by saying prayers which you did not feel; you have been a hypocrite and joined with God's people in singing my praises when you did not praise me in your heart.' I thought he would chide me and bring ten thousand sins to my remembrance. Instead of that, it took only a word, and it was all done. I looked to him, the burden was gone. I could have sung,

'Hosanna! Blessed is he that cometh in the name of the Lord, with pardon in his right hand and acceptance in his left, with abundant blessings to the least deserving of the sons of men.' Now, I have to tell you that Jesus Christ still has the same ability to save as he had when he walked on earth. He ever lives to make intercession for sinners. He is therefore able to save those who come to him: and it is still true that he who comes will not be cast out. There has never been an instance of a man who trusted Christ and perished, and there never shall be an instance.

Do not delay in trusting Christ. Do not entertain a hope that it will ever be easier to trust Jesus than it is now. Do not think that you will ever be in a better state for coming to him than you are in now. The best state in all the world for washing is to be filthy; the best state in all the world to obtain help from a physician is to be terribly sick; the best state for asking for alms is to be a beggar. Do not try to patch up those rags, nor to improve your character, nor to make yourself better before you come to Christ. Come in all your poverty and vileness, just as you are, and say to him, 'My Lord and my God, you have suffered as a man for all the sins of all those who trust you: I trust you; accept me, give me peace and joy.'

And tell the world, I ask you, whether he accepts you or not. If he casts you away, you will be the very first—then let us know about it; but if he receives you, you will be only one among ten thousand who have been accepted—then publish it so that our faith may be confirmed.

Never be content with merely coming close to Christ. When there is a gracious season in a church, and people are converted, many others rest satisfied because they have been in the congregation where works of mercy have been performed. It is dreadful to reflect that there are in our churches men and women who are perfectly satisfied with having spent Sunday in a place of worship. Now, suppose a man has leprosy and he goes to the place where Jesus is: he sees the people thronging to get near, and he joins the press; he pushes on for a certain length of time, and then he returns home perfectly content because he has joined the crowd. The next day the great Master is dispensing healing virtue right and left, and this same man joins the throng, and once more elbows himself tolerably near to the Saviour, and then retires. 'Well,' he says, 'I got into the crowd; I pressed and squeezed, and made my way, and so I was in the way, perhaps I might have got a blessing.' Now that would be precisely similar to the condition of hundreds and thousands of people who go to a place of worship on Sunday. There is the gospel; they come to hear it; they come next Sunday, there is the gospel again; they listen to it, and they go their way each time. 'Fool!' you say to the man with leprosy, 'Why, you did nothing; getting into the crowd was nothing; if you did not touch the Lord who dispensed the healing, you lost all your time; and besides, you incurred responsibility because you got near to him, and yet for not putting out your hand to touch him, you lost the opportunity.' It is the same for you, good people, who go where Jesus Christ is faithfully preached. You come and go, and come and go continually; and what fools you are, what gross fools, to get into the throng and to be satisfied with that, and never touch Christ! Tell me of your church-goings and your chapel-goings! They are not a morsel of use to you unless you touch the Saviour through them.

I must caution you not to be content with touching those who are healed. There are many in the crowd who, having touched the Master, clapped their hands and said, 'Glory be to God, my withered arm is restored,' 'My eyes are opened,' 'My dropsy has vanished,' 'My palsy is gone.' One after another they praise God for his great wonders; and sometimes their friends who were sick would go away with them and say, 'What a mercy! Let us go home together'. They would hear all about it, and talk about it, and tell it to others;

[14]

but all the while, though they rejoiced in the good that was done to others, and sympathized in it, they never touched Jesus for themselves. Noah's carpenters built the ark, but were all drowned. Oh, I beseech you, do not be satisfied with talking about revivals, and hearing about conversions; get an interest in them. Let nothing content any one of us but actual spiritual contact with the Lord Jesus Christ. Let us never sleep or slumber until we have really looked to that great sacrifice which God has lifted up for the sins of men. Let us not think of Christ as another man's Saviour, but be passionately in earnest till we get him for our own.

A young man once said to me, 'I want to know what I must do to be saved.' I reminded him of that verse,

> A guilty, weak, and helpless worm,
> On Thy kind arms I fall.

He said, 'Sir, I cannot fall.' 'Oh,' I said, 'you do not understand me. I do not mean a fall which demands any strength in you; I mean a fall caused by the absence of all strength.' It is to tumble down into Christ's arms because you cannot stand upright. Faint into the arms of Christ; that is faith. Just give up doing, give up depending upon anything that you are, or do, or ever hope to be, and depend upon the complete merits, and finished work, and precious blood of Jesus Christ. If you do this you are saved.

Anything of your own doing spoils it all. You must not have a jot or a tittle of your own; you must give up relying upon your prayers, your tears, your baptism, your repentance, and even your faith itself. Your reliance is to be on nothing but that which is in Jesus Christ. Those dear hands, those blessed feet, are ensigns of his love—look to them. That bleeding, martyred, murdered person is the grand display of the heart of the ever blessed God. Look to it. Look to the Saviour's pangs, griefs and groans. These are punishments for human sin. This is God's wrath spending itself on

[15]

Christ instead of spending itself on the believer. Believe in Jesus, and it is certain that he suffered this for you. Trust in him to save you, and you are saved.

4

Still No Light, and Why?

It shall be my happy task to endeavour to assist into the light those who want to flee from the darkness. We will do so by trying to answer the query, 'How is it that I, wanting light, have not found it yet? Why am I left to grope like a blind man for the wall, and stumble at noon as if it were the night? Why has the Lord not revealed himself to me?' You may have been seeking the light in the wrong place. Many, like Mary, seek the living among the dead. It is possible that you may have been the victim of the false doctrine that peace with God can be found in the use of ceremonies.

It is possible, too, that you have been looking for salvation in the mere belief of a certain creed. You have thought that if you could discover pure orthodoxy, and could then consign your soul into its mould, you would be a saved man; and you have consequently believed unreservedly, as far as you have been able to do so, the set of truths which have been handed to you by the tradition of your ancestors. It may be that your creed is Calvinistic, it is possible that it is Arminian, it may be Protestant, it may be Romish, it may be truth, it may be a lie; but, believe me, solid peace with God is not to be found through the mere reception of any creed, however true or scriptural. Mere head-notion is not the road to heaven. 'Ye must be born again' means a good deal more than you must believe certain dogmas. It is of the utmost possible importance, I grant you, that you should search the Scriptures, for in them you think you have eternal life; but recollect how our

[17]

Lord upbraided the Pharisees. He told them that they searched the Scriptures, but he added, 'Ye will not come to *Me* that ye might have life' (*John* 5:40). You stop short at the Scriptures, and therefore short of eternal life. The study of these, good as it is, cannot save you; you must press beyond this—you must come to the living, personal Christ, once crucified, but now living to plead at the right hand of God, or else your acceptance of the soundest creed cannot effect the salvation of your soul. You may be misled in some other manner; some other mistaken way of seeking peace may have beguiled you, and if so, I earnestly pray that you may see the mistake.

You must understand that there is only one door to salvation, and that is Christ; there is one way, and that is Christ; one truth, and that is Christ; one life, and that is Christ. Salvation lies in Jesus only; it does not lie in you, in your doings, or your feelings, or your knowings, or your resolutions. In *him* all life and light for the sons of men are stored up by the mercy of God the Father. This may be one reason why you have not found the light; because you have sought it in the wrong place.

It is possible that you may have sought it in the wrong spirit. When we ask for pardon, reconciliation and salvation we must remember to whom we speak, and who we are who ask the favour. Some appear to deal with God as if he were bound to give them salvation; as if salvation indeed were the inevitable result of a round of performances, or the deserved reward of a certain amount of virtue. They refuse to see that salvation is a pure gift of God, not of works, not the result of merit, but of free favour only; not of man, neither by man, but of the Lord alone. Though the Lord has placed it on record in his Word, in the plainest language, that 'it is not of him that willeth, nor of him that runneth, but of God that showeth mercy' (*Rom.* 9:16) yet most men in their hearts imagine that everlasting life is tied to duties and earned by

[18]

service. You must abandon such vainglorious notions; you must come before God as a humble petitioner, pleading the promises of mercy, abhorring all idea of merit, confessing that if the Lord condemns you he has a right to do it, and if he saves you, it will be an act of pure gratuitous mercy, a deed of sovereign grace. Oh, too many of you seekers hold your heads too high; to enter the lowly gate of light you must stoop. On the bended knee is the penitent's true place. 'God be merciful to me, a sinner', is the penitent's true prayer. If God should condemn you, you could never complain of injustice, for you have deserved it a thousand times; and if those prayers of yours were never answered, if no mercy ever came, you could not accuse the Lord, for you have no right to be heard. He could righteously withhold an answer of peace if he so willed.

Confess that you are an undeserving, ill-deserving, hell-deserving sinner and begin to pray as you have never prayed before. Cry out of the depths of self-abasement if you want to be heard. Come as a beggar, not as a creditor. Come to crave, not to demand. Use only this argument, 'Lord, hear me, for you are gracious, and Jesus died; I cry to you as a condemned criminal who seeks pardon. Deliver me from going down into the pit, that I may praise your name.' This harbouring of a proud spirit, I fear, has been a great source of mischief with many, and if it has been so with you, amend it and go now with humble and contrite hearts, in lowliness and broken-ness of spirit, to your Father whom you have offended, for he will surely accept you as his children.

Others have not obtained peace, I fear, because they do not yet have a clear idea of the true way of finding it. Although it has been preached to us so often, it is still little understood. The way of peace with God is seen through a haze by most men, so that no matter how plainly you put it, they will, if it is possible, misunderstand you. Your salvation does not depend upon what you do, but upon what Christ did when he

[19]

offered himself as a sacrifice for sin. All your salvation takes root in the death throes of Calvary; the great Substitute bore your sin and suffered its penalty. Your sin shall never destroy you if upon that bloody tree the Lord's chosen High Priest made a full expiation for your sins; they shall not be laid against you any more forever. What you have to do is simply to accept what Jesus has finished. I know your idea is that you are to bring something to him; but that vainglorious idea has ruined many, and will ruin more. When you are brought empty-handed, made willing to accept a free and full salvation from the hand of the Crucified, then, and then only, will you be saved.

There is life for a look at the Crucified One.

But men will not look to the cross. No, they conspire to raise another cross; or they aspire to adorn that cross with jewels; or they labour to wreathe it with sweet flowers; but they will not give a simple look to the Saviour, and rely alone on him. Yet no soul can ever obtain peace with God by any other means; while this means is so effectual that it has never failed, and never shall.

The waters of Abana and Pharpar are preferred by proud human nature, but the waters of Jordan alone can take away the leprosy (see *2 Kings* 5:1–14). Our repentings, our doings, our resolutions, these are simply broken cisterns; but the only life-draught is to be found in the fountain of living water opened up by our Immanuel's death. Do you understand that a simple trust, a sincere dependence, a hearty reliance upon Christ is the way of salvation? If you do know this, may the God who taught you to understand the way give you grace to run in it, and then your light has come; arise and shine. Your peace has come, for Christ has bought it with his blood. For as many as trust in him he has been punished; their sins are gone:

> Lost as in a shoreless flood,
> Drown'd in the Redeemer's blood;
> Pardon'd soul, how bless'd art thou,
> Justified from all things now.

If none of these arguments have touched your case, let me further suggest that perhaps you have not found light because you have sought it in a half-hearted manner. None enter heaven who are only half-inclined to go there. Cold prayers ask God to refuse them. When a man manifestly does not value the mercy which he asks, and would be perfectly content not to receive it, it is small wonder if he is denied. Many a sinner lies, year after year, freezing outside the door of God's mercy, because he has never thoroughly bestirred himself to take the kingdom of heaven by violence. If you are willing to be unsaved, you shall be left to perish; but if you are inwardly set and resolved that you will give God no rest until you win a pardon from him, he will give you your heart's desire. The man who must be saved, shall be. The man whose heart is set on finding the way to Zion's hill, shall find that way. I believe that usually a sense of our pardon comes to us when, Samson-like, we grasp the posts of mercy's door with desperate vehemence, as though we would pluck them up, post and bar and all, rather than remain shut out any longer from peace and safety. Strong crying and tears, groanings of spirit, vehement longings, and ceaseless pleadings—these are the weapons which, through the blood of Jesus, win us the victory in our warfare of seeking the Lord. Perhaps, then, you have not bestirred yourself as you should have done. May the Lord help you to be a mighty wrestler and then a prevailing prince!

5

'We Wait for Light'

Isaiah 59:9

I address those who sincerely want to obtain the true and heavenly light, who have waited hoping to receive it, but instead of obtaining it are in a worse, at least in a sadder, state than they were. They are almost driven into the dark foreboding that for them no light will ever come, they shall be prisoners chained forever in the valley of the shadow of death. These people are in some degree aware of their natural darkness. They are looking for light. They are not content with their obscurity, they are waiting for brightness. There are a few who are not content to be what their first birth has made them; they discover in their nature much evil and would be glad to get rid of it; they find in their understanding much ignorance, and they long to be illuminated; they do not understand Scripture when they read it, and though they hear gospel terms, they still fail to grasp gospel-thought. They pant to escape from this ignorance, they desire to know the truth which saves the soul; and their desire is not only to know it in theory, but to know it by its practical power upon their inner selves. They really and anxiously want to be delivered from the state of nature, which they feel to be a dangerous one, and to be brought into the glorious liberty of the children of God.

Oh, these are the best kind of hearers, these in whom right desires have begun to be awakened. Men who are dissatisfied with the darkness are evidently not altogether dead, for the dead shall slumber in the catacombs, heedless as to whether it is noon or night. Such men evidently have not fallen completely asleep, for they who slumber sleep better because of the darkness; they ask for no sunbeams to molest their dreams. Such people are evidently not completely blind, because it makes no difference to the blind whether the sun floods the landscape with glory, or night conceals it with her black veil. Those to whom our thoughts are directly turned are somewhat awakened, aroused and bestirred, and this is no small blessing for, alas, most people are a stolid mass regarding spiritual things, and the preacher might almost as hopefully strive to create a soul within the ribs of death, or extort warm tears of pity from Sicilian marble, as evoke spiritual emotions from the people of this generation. So these people are hopeful in their condition who, just as the trees twist their branches towards the sunlight, they long after Jesus, the light and life of men.

Moreover, these persons have a high idea of what the light is. They call it *brightness*. They wait for it, and are grieved because it does not come. If you greatly value spiritual life you have not made a mistake; if you count it a priceless thing to obtain an interest in Christ, the forgiveness of your sins, and peace with God, you judge according to solemness. You shall never exaggerate in your valuation of the one thing necessary. It is true that those who trust in God are a happy people; it is true that to be brought into sonship, and adopted into the family of the great God, is a boon for which kings might well exchange their diadems. You cannot think too highly of the blessings of grace; I would rather incite in you a sacred covetousness after them than in the remotest degree lower your estimate of their preciousness. Salvation is such a blessing that heaven hangs upon it; if you win grace you have the germ of heaven within you, the security, the pledge and earnest of everlasting bliss. So far, again, there is much that is hopeful in you. It is good that you loathe the darkness and prize the light.

The people I want to speak with have some hope that they may yet obtain this light; in fact, they are waiting for it, hopefully waiting, and are somewhat disappointed that after waiting for the light, instead, obscurity has come. They are evidently astonished at the failure of their hopes. They are amazed to find themselves walking in darkness, when they had fondly hoped that the candle of the Lord would shine round about them. I would encourage in you that spark of hope, for despair is one of the most terrible hindrances to the reception of the gospel. So long as awakened sinners cherish a hope of mercy, we have hope for them. We hope, O seeker, that before long you will be able to sing of pardon bought with blood, and when this scene is closed, shall enter through the gates into the pearly city amongst the blessed who forever see the face of the well-beloved. Though it may seem too good to be true, yet even you, in your calmer moments, think that one day you will rejoice that Christ is yours, and take your seat amongst his people, though the poorest of them all in your own estimation. Then you imagine in your heart how fervently you will love your Redeemer, how rapturously you will kiss the very dust of his feet, how gratefully you will bless him who has lifted the poor from the dunghill and set him among princes. May you no longer look through the window wistfully at the banquet, but come in to sit at the table, and feed upon Christ, rejoicing with his chosen!

The people I am describing are those who have learned to plead their case with God. 'We wait for light, but only see obscurity; for brightness, but we walk in darkness.' It is a declaration of inward feelings, a laying bare of the heart's agonies to the Most High. Although you have not yet found the peace you seek, it is good that you have begun to pray. Perhaps you think it is poor praying; indeed, you hardly care to call it prayer at all; but God does not judge as you do. A groan is heard in heaven; a deep-fetched sigh and a falling tear are prevalent weapons at the throne of God. Yes, your

soul cries to God, and you cannot help it. When you are about
your daily work you find yourself sighing, 'Oh, that my load
of guilt were gone! Oh, that I could call the Lord my Father
with an unfaltering tongue!' Night after night and day after
day this desire rises from you like the morning mist from the
valleys. You would tear off your right arm, and pluck out
your right eye, if you might gain the unspeakable benefit of
salvation in Jesus Christ. You are sincerely anxious for reconciliation with God, and your anxiety reveals itself in prayer
and supplication. I hope these prayers will continue. I trust
you will never cease your crying. May the Holy Spirit const-
rain you to continue to sigh and groan. Like the importunate
woman (*Luke* 18:1–8), may you press your case until the gracious answer is granted through the merits of Jesus. So far
things are hopeful for you; but when I say hopeful, I wish I
could say much more, for mere hopefulness is not enough. It
is not enough to desire, it is not enough to seek, it is not
enough to pray; you must actually obtain, you must actually
lay hold on eternal life. You will never enjoy comfort and
peace till you have passed out of the merely hopeful stage into
a better and a brighter one, by making sure of your interest in
the Lord Jesus by a living, appropriating faith. In the exalted
Saviour all the gifts and graces which you need are stored up,
in readiness to supply your wants. Oh, may you come to his
fullness, and out of it receive grace for grace!

The person I wish to comfort may be described by one
other touch of the pen. He is one who is *quite willing to lay
bare his heart before God*, to confess his desires, whether right
or wrong, and to expose his condition, whether unhealthy or
sound. While we try to cloak anything from God, we are both
wicked and foolish. It shows a rebellious spirit when we have
a desire to hide away from our Maker; but when a man
uncovers his wound, invites inspection of its sore, bids the
surgeon cut away the leprous film which covered its corrup-
tion, and says to him, 'Here, probe into its depths, see what

evil there is in it; do not spare me, but make a sure cure of the wound,' then he is in a fair way to be recovered. When a man is willing to make God his confessor, and freely, and without hypocrisy, pours out his heart like water before the Lord, there is hope for him. You have told the Lord your position, you have spread your petitions before him—I trust you will continue to do so until you find relief; but I have yet a higher hope, namely, that you may soon obtain peace with God through Jesus Christ our Lord.

6

The Invitation

Do you desire eternal life? Is there within your soul a hunger-
ing and a thirsting after such things that may satisfy your
spirit and make you live forever? Then 'Come, for now *all
things* are ready' (*Luke* 14:17)—all, not some, but all. There
is nothing that you need between here and heaven which is
not provided in Jesus Christ, in his person and in his work.
All things are ready: life for your death, forgiveness for your
sin, cleansing for your filth, clothing for your nakedness, joy
for your sorrow, strength for your weakness, indeed, more
than anything you could ever want is stored up in the boundless nature and work of Christ. You must not say, 'I cannot
come because I do not have this, or do not have that.' Are you
to prepare the feast? Are you to provide anything? Are you
bringing even salt or water? You do not know your true condition, or you would not dream of such a thing. The great
householder himself has provided the whole of the feast, you
have nothing to do with the provision but to enjoy it. If you
lack anything, come and take what you lack; the greater your
need the greater is the reason why you should come where all
things that your need can possibly want will be at once
supplied. If you are so needy that you have nothing good at
all about you, all things are ready. When God has provided
all things, what more could you possibly provide? It would
be a disgraceful insult if you thought of adding to his 'all
things'; it would be a presumptuous competing with the provisions of the Great King, and this he will not endure. All that

you are lacking between the gates of hell, where you now lie, and the gates of heaven, to which grace will bring you if you believe—all is provided and prepared in Jesus Christ the Saviour.

And all things are *ready*. Dwell on that word. The oxen and the fatlings were killed; and what is more, they were prepared to be eaten, they were ready to be feasted on, they smoked on the board. It is something when the king gives orders for the slaughter of so many bullocks for the feast, but the feast is not ready then; and when the victims fall beneath the axe, and they are stripped and hung up ready for the fire, something has been done, but they are still not ready. It is only when the joints are served hot and steaming upon the table, and everything else that is wanted is brought out and laid in proper order for the banquet that all things are ready, and this is the case now. At this very moment you will find the feast is in the best possible condition; it was never better and never can be better than it is now. All things are ready, in the exact condition that you need them to be, in exactly the right condition that is best for your soul's comfort and enjoyment. All things are ready; nothing needs to be further mellowed or sweetened, everything is as perfect as eternal love can make it.

But notice the word 'now'. 'All things are *now* ready'—just now, at this moment. At feasts, you know, the good housewife is often troubled if the guests come late. She would be sorry if they came half an hour too soon, but half an hour too late spoils everything, and she is in a great state of fret and worry when all things are ready yet her friends still delay. Leave food in the oven awhile, and it does not seem to be 'now ready', but more than ready, and even spoiled. So the great householder lays stress upon this, all things are *now* ready, therefore come at once.

He does not say that if you delay for another seven years all things will then be ready: God grant that long before that

space of time you may have got beyond the need to be persuaded to become a taster of the feast, but he says that everything is ready now, just now. Just now that your heart is so
heavy and your mind is so careless, that your spirit is so
wandering—all things are ready now.

If the reason why a sinner is to come is because all things
are ready, then it is idle for him to say, 'But I am not ready.'
It is clear that all the readiness required on man's part is a willingness to come and receive the blessing which God has provided. There is nothing else necessary; if men are willing to
come, they may come, they will come. Where the Lord has
been pleased to touch the will so that man has a desire
towards Christ, where the heart really hungers and thirsts
after righteousness, that is all the readiness which is wanted.
All the fitness he requires is that first you feel your need of
him (and that he gives you), and that secondly, in feeling
your need of him you are willing to come to him. Willingness
to come is everything. A readiness to believe in Jesus, a willingness to cast the soul on him, a preparedness to accept him
just as he is, because you feel that he is just the Saviour that
you need—that is all: there was no other readiness, there
could have been none, in the case of those who were poor and
blind, and lame and maimed, yet came to the feast. The text
does not say, 'You are ready, therefore come'; that is a legal
way of putting the gospel; but it says, 'All things are ready,
the gospel is ready, therefore you are to come.' As for *your*
readiness, all the readiness that is possibly wanted is a readiness which the Spirit gives us—namely, willingness to come
to Jesus.

Now notice that the unreadiness of those who were asked
arose out of their possessions and out of their abilities. One
would not come because he had bought a piece of land. What
a great heap Satan casts up between the soul and the Saviour!
With worldly possessions and good deeds he builds an earth-
work of huge dimensions between the sinner and his Lord.

[29]

Some gentlemen have too many acres ever to come to Christ: they think too much of the world to think much of him. Many have too many fields of good works in which there are growing crops on which they pride themselves, and these cause them to feel that they are persons of great importance. Many a man cannot come to Christ for all things because he has so much already.

Others could not come because they had so much to do, and could do it well—one had bought five yoke of oxen and he was going to prove them. He was a strong man well able to plow; the reason why he did not come was because he had so much ability. Thousands are kept away from grace by what they have and by what they can do. Emptiness is more preparatory to a feast than fullness. How often does it happen that poverty and inability help to lead the soul to Christ. When a man thinks he is rich he will not come to the Saviour. When a man dreams that he is able at any time to repent and believe, and to do everything for himself that is wanted, he is not likely to come and by a simple faith repose in Christ. It is not what you have not but what you have that keeps many of you from Christ. Sinful Self is a devil, but Righteous Self is seven devils. The man who feels himself guilty may for a while be kept away by his guilt, but the man who is self-righteous will never come; until the Lord has taken his pride away from him he will still refuse the feast of free grace. The possession of abilities and honours and riches keeps men from coming to the Redeemer.

But on the other hand, personal condition does not constitute an unfitness for coming to Christ, for the sad condition of those who became guests did not debar them from the supper. Some were *poor*, and doubtless wretched and ragged; they did not have a penny to bless themselves with, as we say. Their garments were tattered, perhaps worse, they were filthy; they were not fit to be near respectable people, they would certainly be no credit to my Lord's table; but those who went to bring them in did not search their pockets, nor look at their coats, but they fetched them in. They were poor, but the messengers were told to bring in the poor, and therefore they brought them. Their poverty did not prevent their being ready; and Oh, poor soul, if you are poor literally, or poor spiritually, neither sort of poverty constitutes an unfitness for divine mercy. If you are brought to your last penny, or even if that penny is spent and you have pawned everything you have, yet are still up to your eyes in debt and think that there is nothing left for you but to be laid by the heels in prison forever, nevertheless you may come, poverty and all.

Another class of them were *maimed*, and so were not very attractive in appearance: an arm had been lopped off, or an eye had been gouged out. One had lost a nose, and another a leg. They were in all stages and shapes of dismemberment. Sometimes we turn our heads away, and feel that we would rather give anything than look upon beggars who show their wounds, and describe how they were maimed. But it did not matter how badly they were disfigured; they were brought in, and not one of them was repulsed because of the ugly cuts he had received. So, poor soul, however Satan may have torn and lopped you, and whatsoever condition he may have brought you to, so that you feel ashamed to live; nevertheless this does not make you unfit for coming, you may come to his table of grace just as you are. Moral disfigurements are soon rectified when Jesus takes the character in hand. Come to him, however sadly you are injured by sin.

There were others who were *lame*. They had lost a leg, or it was of no use to them, and they could not come except with the help of a crutch; but nevertheless that was no reason why they were not welcome. Ah, if you find it difficult to believe, that is no reason why you should not come and receive the grand absolution which Jesus Christ is ready to bestow upon you. Lame with doubting and distrusting, nevertheless come to the supper and say, 'Lord, I believe; help my unbelief.'

Others were *blind*, and when they were told to come they could not see the way, but in that case the messenger was not told to tell them to come, he was commanded to bring them, and a blind man can come if he is brought. All that was wanted was willingness to be led by the hand in the right direction. Now you who cannot fully understand the gospel as you wish to do, who are puzzled and muddled, put your hand into the hand of Jesus, and be willing to believe what you cannot comprehend, and to grasp in confidence that which you are not yet able to measure with your understanding. The blind, however ignorant or uninstructed they are, shall not be kept away because of that.

Then there were the men in the *highways*, I suppose they were beggars; and the men in the *hedges*, I suppose they were hiding, and were probably thieves; but nevertheless they were told to come, and though they were highwaymen and hedge-birds, even that did not prevent their coming and finding welcome. Though outcasts, spiritual gypsies, people that nobody cared for; whatever they might be, that was not the question, they were to come because all things were ready. Come in rags, come in filth, come maimed, come covered with sores, come in all sorts of filthiness and abomination, yet because all things are ready they were to be brought or to be compelled to come in.

I think it was the very thing, which in any one of these people looked like unfitness, which was a help to them. It is a great truth that what we regard as unfitness is often our truest fitness. I want you to notice these poor, blind and lame people. Some of those who were invited would not come because they had bought some land, or five yoke of oxen, but when the messenger went up to the poor man in rags and said, 'Come to the supper,' it is quite clear he would not say he had bought a field, or oxen, for he could not do it, he did not have a penny to do the thing with, so he was delivered from that temptation. And when a man is invited to come to

Christ and he says, 'I do not want him, I have a righteousness of my own,' he will stay away; but when the Lord Jesus
came along to me I was never tempted in that way, because
I had no righteousness of my own, and could not have made
one if I had tried. I know some who could not patch up a
garment of righteousness if they were to put all their rags
together, and this is a great help to their receiving the Lord
Jesus. What a blessedness it is to have such a sense of soul-
poverty that you will never stay away from Christ because of
what you possess.

Some could not come because they had married a wife.
Now I think it very likely that those people who were
maimed and cut about were so injured that they had no wife,
and perhaps could not get anybody to have them. Well then,
they did not have that temptation to stay away. They were
too maimed to attract the eye of anybody who was looking for
beauty, and therefore they were not tempted that way. But
they found at the ever-blessed supper of the Lamb an everlasting wedlock which was infinitely better. Thus do souls
lose earthly joys and comforts, and by the loss they gain sup-
remely: they are therefore made willing to close in with
Christ and find a higher comfort and a higher joy. That
maiming which looked like unfitness turned out to be fitness.

One excuse made was, 'I have bought five yoke of oxen,
and I go to prove them.' The lame could not do that. When
the messenger touched the lame man on the shoulder and
said, 'Come', he could not say, 'I am going out tonight to
plow with my new teams.' He had never been over the fields
since he had lost his leg, so he could not make such an excuse.
The blind man could not say, 'I have bought a piece of land
and I must go to see it'; he was free from all the lusts of the
eye, and so was all the more ready to be led to the supper.
When a soul feels its own sinfulness, and wretchedness and
lost estate, it thinks itself unfit to come to Christ, but this is
an assistance to it, since it prevents its looking to anything

else but Christ, kills its excuses, and makes it free to accept salvation by grace.

But how about the men that were in the highway? Well, it seems to me that they were already on the road, and at least out of their houses, if they had any. If they were out there begging, they were more ready to accept an invitation to a meal of victuals, for it was that they were singing for. A man who is out of the house of his own self-righteousness, though he be a great sinner, is in a more favourable position and more likely to come to Christ than he who prides himself on his supposed self-righteousness.

7

Something to be Set Right

When a man does wrong, and yet will not confess it, how wrong he must be! Or when, having confessed it, he does not feel proper shame; or after feeling ashamed for a while he returns to the same evil like the dog to his vomit, how deep must the evil be in his moral nature, how trebly diseased he must be, inasmuch as he does not feel sin to be sin at all! When a man has done wrong and knows it, and stands with bitter repentance to confess the evil, why, you think hopefully of him; after all, there are good points about the man; there is a vitality in him that will throw out the disease. But when the villain, having perpetrated a grave and causeless offence, does not for a moment acknowledge he has done wrong, but continues calmly to perpetrate the offence again; ah, then, where is there any good in him? Is he not thoroughly bad? Now, you are like that.

If you were at all right with God, you would fall at your Father's feet, and never rise until you were forgiven; your tears would flow day and night until you had the assurance of pardon. But since your heart seems to yourself to be made of hell-hardened steel, and to be like a millstone that feels nothing, then there is need for healing, and you seem the very man whom Christ came to save, for he came not to call the righteous but sinners to repentance, not to save those who had no need for healing but to heal those like you, whose need is desperate indeed.

As if to prove your own need of healing, you are, according

to your own statement, *unable to pray*. You have been trying to pray lately, and wished you could. You put yourself upon your knees, but your heart does not talk with God; a horrible dread comes over you, or else frivolous and vain thoughts distract you. 'Oh,' you have said, 'I would give a thousand pounds for one tear of repentance; I would be ready to pluck out my eyes if I could call upon God as the poor publican did, with "God be merciful to me a sinner". I once thought it the easiest thing in the world once to pray, but now I find that a true prayer is beyond my power.' You do need healing indeed, possessed with a dumb devil, and all your other devils also, and unable to cry out for mercy; yours is a sad case. You need healing, and I cannot help repeating to you, 'He healed them that had need of healing'; why should he not heal you?

Ah, but you tell me your feelings, your desires after good things are very often damped. Perhaps you are sincerely in earnest, but tomorrow you may be just as careless as ever. The other day you went into your chamber and wrestled with God, but a temptation came across your path, and you were as thoughtless about divine things as if you had never been aroused to a sense of their value. Ah! this shows your need for healing. You are vile indeed when you dare to trifle with eternity, to sport with death and judgment, and to be at ease while in danger of hell—your heart indeed needs healing; and though I grieve that you should be in such a plight, yet I rejoice that I am able to add, 'He healed those who had need of healing.'

Though you know your case is bad, at times you set up a kind of self-repentance and try to justify yourself in the sight of God. You say, 'I have repented, or tried to do so; I have prayed, or tried to pray; I have done all I can to be saved, and God will not save me.' That is to say, you throw the blame of your damnation upon God, and make yourself out to be righteous in his sight. You know this is wrong. If you are not

[36]

saved, it is because you will not believe in Jesus. There is the only hitch and the only difficulty. Your damnation is not of God, but of yourself; it is necessitated by your own wilful wickedness in not believing in Christ; but inasmuch as you are so wicked as to dare to excuse yourself, you do need healing, you do urgently need to be saved. But, then, the minute that you have thus excused yourself, you rush to the opposite extreme; you declare that you have sinned past hope, that you deserve to be now in hell, and that God can never forgive you. You deny the mercy of God, you deny the power of Christ to forgive you and cleanse you; you fly in the face of God's Word, and you make him out to be a liar.

When he tells you that if you trust Jesus you shall find peace, you tell him it is not possible there can be any peace to you; when he reminds you that he never rejected one, you insinuate that he will reject you; you thus insult the Divine Majesty by denying the truthfulness and honesty of God. You do need healing when you allow wicked despair to get the mastery of you like this; you are far gone, very far gone, but I rejoice to know that you are still among those Jesus is able to heal. He came to those who needed healing, and you cannot deny you are one of those. Why, even Satan himself will not have the impudence to tell you that you have no need of healing. Oh, if only you would cast yourself into the Saviour's arms—not trying to make yourself out to be good, but acknowledging all that I have laid to your charge, and then, trusting as a sinner to that Lamb of God that takes away the sin of the world.

Remember you need healing, for unless you are healed of these sins, and of all these wicked tendencies and thoughts, as sure as you are a living man you will be cast into hell. I know of no truth that ever causes me such pain to preach as this, not that sinners will be damned, awful though the truth of that is, but that *awakened* sinners will be damned unless they believe in Jesus. You must not make a Christ out of your tears, you must not hope to find safety in your bitter thoughts and cruel despairs. Unless you believe you shall never be established. Unless you come to Christ, you may be convinced of sin, of righteousness and judgment too, but those convictions will only be preludes to your destruction. You call yourself a seeker, but until you are a finder you are an enemy to God, and God is angry with you every day. I have no alternative for you, however tender and broken-hearted you may be, but this one—believe and live; refuse to believe, and you must perish, for your broken-heartedness, and tears, and professed contrition can never stand in the place of Christ. You must have faith in Jesus, or you must die eternally.

I need not enter into what your case is. Remember, Jesus has saved a parallel case to yours. Yours may seem to yourself to be exceedingly odd, but somewhere or other in the New Testament you will find one as singular as yours. You tell me that you are full of so much wickedness. Did he not cast seven devils out of Mary Magdalen? Yes, but your wickedness seems to be greater than even seven devils. Did he not drive a whole legion of devils out of the demoniac of Gadara? You tell me that you cannot pray, but he healed one possessed of a dumb devil; you feel hardened and insensible, but he cast out a deaf devil. You tell me you cannot believe; neither could the man with the withered arm stretch it out, but he did it when Jesus ordered him to. You tell me you are dead in sin, but Jesus made even the dead live. Your case cannot be so bad that it has not been matched, and Christ has conquered something like it.

Remember again, Christ can save you, for there is no record in the world, nor has there ever been handed down to us by tradition a single case in which Jesus has failed. If I could meet anywhere in my wanderings a soul which had cast itself on Christ alone, and yet had received no pardon— if there could be found in hell a solitary spirit that relied upon the precious blood and found no salvation, then the gospel might well be laid by in the dark, and no longer gloried in; but as that has not happened, and never shall happen, sinner, you shall not be the first exception. If you come to Christ—and to come to him is only to trust him wholly and simply—you cannot perish, for he has said, 'Him that cometh to me I will in nowise cast out.' Will he prove a liar? Will you dare think so? O come, for he cannot cast you out. Think for a moment, sinner, and this may comfort you: he whom I preach to you as the healer of your soul is God. What can be impossible with God? What sin cannot he forgive who is God over all? If your transgressions were to be dealt with by an angel, they might surpass all Gabriel's power; but it is Immanuel, God with us, who has come to save.

Moreover, you cannot doubt his will. Have you heard of him—he who was God and became man?

> He was as gentle as a woman,
> His heart is made of tenderness,
> It overflows with love.

It was not in him to be harsh. When the woman found in the very act of adultery was brought to him, what did he say? 'Neither do I condemn thee, go and sin no more.' It was said of him, 'This man receiveth sinners, and eateth with them,' and he is not changed now that he reigns above; he is just as willing to receive sinners now as when he was here below.

Was the atonement a fiction? Was the death of the eternal Son of God ineffectual? There must be power enough there to take away sin. Come and wash, come and wash, you who are vile and stained with sin, come and wash, and you shall find instant cleansing the moment that by faith you touch his purifying blood.

Jesus demands your trust. He deserves it, let him have it. You need healing; he came to heal those who need healing: he can heal you. What is to be done in order that you may be healed, that all your sins may be forgiven and yourself saved? All that is to be done is to leave off your own doing, and let him do for you; leave off looking to yourself, or looking to others, and just come and cast yourself on him.

'Oh,' you say, 'but I cannot believe.' Cannot believe! Then do you know what you are doing? You are making him a liar. If you tell a man, 'I cannot believe you', that is only another way of saying, 'You are a liar.' Oh, you will not dare say that of Christ. No, my friend, I take you by the hand and say another word—*you must believe him.* He is God, dare you doubt him? He died for sinners. Can you doubt the power of his blood? He has promised. Will you insult him by mistrusting his word? 'Oh, no,' you say, 'I feel I must believe, I must trust him; but suppose that trust of mine should not be of the right kind? Suppose it should be a natural trust?' Ah, my friend, a humble trust in Jesus is a thing that never grew in natural ground. For a poor soul to come and trust in Christ is always the fruit of the Spirit. You need not raise a question about that. Never did the devil, never did mere nature empty a man of himself and bring him to Jesus. Do not be anxious on that point. 'But', says one, 'the Spirit must lead me to believe him!' Yes, but you cannot see the Spirit; his work is a secret and a mystery. What you have to do is to believe in Jesus; there he stands, God and yet a suffering man, making atonement, and he tells you if you trust him you shall be saved. You must trust him; you cannot doubt him. Why should you? What has he done that should make you doubt him?

> O believe the record true,
> God to you his Son has given.

And if you trust him, you need not raise the question as to where your faith came from. It must have come from the Holy Spirit, who is not seen in his workings, for he works where he chooses. You see the fruit of his work, and that is enough for you. Do you believe that Jesus is the Christ? If so, you are born of God. If you have cast yourself, sink or swim, on him, then you are saved.

We read how a man was saved from being shot. He had been condemned in a Spanish court, but being an American citizen, and also of English birth, the consuls of the two countries interposed, and declared that the Spanish authorities had no power to put him to death. And what did they do to secure his life? They wrapped him up in their flags, they covered him with the Stars and Stripes and the Union Jack, and defied the executioners. 'Now fire a shot if you dare, for if you do, you defy the nations represented by those flags, and you will bring the powers of those two great nations upon you.' There stood the man, and before him the soldiers, and though a single shot might have ended his life, yet he was as invulnerable as though in a coat of triple steel. In the same way, Jesus Christ has taken my poor guilty soul ever since I believed in him, and has wrapped around me the blood-red flag of his atoning sacrifice, and before God can destroy me, or any other soul that is wrapped in the atonement, he must insult his Son and dishonour this sacrifice; and that he never will do, blessed be his name.

8

Hindrances to Coming to the Light

There may be some sin within you which you are harbouring to your soul's peril. When a soldier's foot has refused to heal, the surgeon has been known to examine it very minutely, and manipulate every part. Each bone is there, and in its place; there is no apparent cause for the inflammation, but yet the wound refuses to heal. The surgeon probes and probes again, until his lancet comes into contact with a hard foreign substance. 'Here it is,' he says, 'a bullet is lodged here; this must come out, or the wound will never close.' So my probe may discover a secret in you, and if so, it must come out, or you must die. You cannot expect to have peace with God, and still indulge in that drunkard's glass. What, a drunkard reconciled to God? You cannot hope to enjoy peace with God, and yet refuse to speak with that relative who offended you years ago. What, look to be forgiven, when you will not yourself forgive? There are doubtful practices in your trade behind the counter; do you dare to hope that God will accept a thief? —for that is what you are, a thief and a liar. You brand your goods dishonestly, call them twenty when they are fifteen; do you expect God to be your friend while you remain a rogue? Do you think he will smile on you in your knavery, and walk with you when you choose dirty ways? Perhaps you indulge a haughty spirit, or it may be an idle disposition; it does not matter which kind of devil is in you, it must come out, or else the peace of God cannot come in. Now, are you willing to give sin up? If not, it is all lost time to preach Christ to you, for he is not meant to be a Saviour of those who persevere in sin. He came to save his people *from* their sins, not *in* them; and if you still cling to a darling sin, do not be deceived, for you can never enter within the gates of heaven.

Why have some not found the light? It may be that you have sought peace with God only occasionally; after an earnest sermon you have been awakened; but when the sermon has been concluded, you have gone back to your slumber like the sluggard who turns again upon his bed. After a sickness, or when there has been a death in the family, you have then zealously bestirred yourself; but before long you have declined into the same carelessness as before. Remember he who wins the race is not the one who runs in spurts, but the one who continues running to the end. No man gets Christ by thinking of him only now and then, and in the mean time regards vanity and falsehood in his heart. He only shall have Christ who must have him, who must have him now, and who gives his whole heart to him, and cries, 'I will seek him till I find him, and when I find him I will never let him go.'

Let me remind you that the great reason why earnest souls do not get speedy rest lies in this: they are disobedient to the one plain gospel precept, 'Believe on the Lord Jesus Christ, and thou shalt be saved.' I would pin them to this point. It is not necessary at all to combat their doubts and fears; we may do it, but I do not know that we are called upon to do so; the plain matter of fact is, God lays down a way of peace, and you will not have it. God says by believing in Jesus you shall live: you will not believe in Christ, and yet hope to live! God reveals to you his dear Son and says, 'Trust him,' and moreover, 'He that believeth not God hath made him a liar' (*1 John* 5:10), and yet you dare to make God a liar; every minute that you live in a state of unbelief, you, as far as you can, make God to be a liar! What an atrocity for any one of us to fall into! What an amazing presumption for a sinner to live in who professes to be seeking peace with God!

I will suppose that I have you by the hand, and am gazing intently into your eyes. I fear for you because of the danger that you will become frost-bitten by your long sorrow, and fall into a fatal slumber. You have been seeking rest, but you have not found it; *what an unhappy state you are in*! You are now unreconciled to God; your sin clamours for punishment; you are among those with whom God is angry every day. Can you bear to be in such a condition? Does something not bid you arise and flee out of this city of destruction in case you are consumed? What happiness you are missing every day! If you lay hold on Christ by faith, you would possess a joy and peace passing all understanding. You are fretting in this low and miserable dungeon; you have been in the dark year after year, when the sun is shining, the sweet flowers are blooming, and everything is waiting to lead you forth with gladness. Oh, what joys you lose by being an unbeliever! Why do you stay so long in this evil state? Meanwhile, what good you might have done! Oh, if you had been led to look to Jesus Christ months ago, instead of sitting in darkness yourself, you would have been leading others to Christ, and pointing other eyes to that dear cross that brought peace to you.

What sin you are daily committing! For you are daily an unbeliever, daily denying the ability of Christ, and so doing injury to his honour. Does the Spirit of God within you not make you say, 'I will arise, and go to my Father'? Oh, if there is such a thought trembling in your soul, do not quench it, obey it, arise and go, and may your Father's arms be wrapped around your neck before today's sun goes down. Meanwhile, permit me to say, what a hardening process is insensibly going on within! If not better, you are certainly worse than twelve months ago. Why, those promises that cheered you then now yield no comfort! Those threats which once startled now cause you no alarm! Will you dawdle any longer? You have waited to be better, and you are growing worse and worse. You have said, 'I will come at a more convenient season', and every season is more inconvenient than the one which came before it. You doubted then—you are the victim of deeper and more dastardly doubts today. Oh, that you could believe in him who must be true! Oh, that you could trust in him who ought to be trusted, for he can never deceive! I pray the day may come, even this very moment, when you will shake yourself from the dust, arise and put on your beautiful garments, for every hour you sit on the dung-hill of your soul-destroying doubts you are being fastened by strong bands of iron to the seat of despair. Your eye is growing dimmer, your hand more palsied; and the poison in your veins is raging more furiously. Yonder is the Saviour's cross, and there is efficacy in his blood for you. Trust Jesus now, and this moment you will enter into peace. The gate of mercy swings readily on its hinge and opens wide to every soul which casts itself upon the bosom of the Saviour. Oh, why are you waiting? Mischief will befall you. The sun is going down; hurry, traveller, in case you are overtaken with ever-lasting night.

There are many people around you, some of whom you may know, who have trusted Jesus and they have found light. They once suffered your disappointments, but they have now found rest to their souls. They came to Jesus just as they were, and at this moment they can tell you that they are satisfied in him. If others have found such peace, why not you? Jesus is still the same. It is not to Christ's advantage to reject a sinner, it is not for God's glory to destroy a seeker; rather, it is for his honour and glory to receive those who humbly rest in the sacrifice of his dear Son. What is holding you back? You are called, come. You are pressed to come, come. In the courts of law I have sometimes heard a man called as a witness, and no sooner is he called, though he may be at the end of the court, than he begins to press his way up to the witness-box. Nobody says, 'Who is this man pushing here?' or, if they should say, 'Who are you?' it would be a sufficient answer to say, 'My name was called.' 'But you are not rich, you have no gold ring upon your finger!' 'No, but that is not it, I was called.' 'But you are not a man of repute, or rank, or character!' 'It does not matter, I was called. Make way.' So make way, doubts and fears; make way, devils of the infernal lake; Christ calls the sinner. Sinner, come. Though you have nothing to recommend you, because it is written, 'Him that cometh unto me I will in no wise cast out,' come, and the Lord will bless you, for Christ's sake.

9

Seekers Encouraged—the Substitute

The whole pith and marrow of the religion of Christianity lies in the doctrine of 'substitution', and I do not hesitate to affirm my conviction that a very large proportion of 'Christians' are not Christians at all, for they do not understand the fundamental doctrine of the Christian creed; and, alas, there are preachers who do not preach, or even believe this cardinal truth. They speak of the blood of Jesus in an indistinct kind of way, and talk about the death of Christ in a hazy style of poetry, but they do not strike this nail on the head, and lay it down that the way of salvation is by Christ's becoming a Substitute for guilty man. This shall make me the more plain and definite. Sin is an accursed thing. God, from the necessity of his holiness, must curse it; he must punish men for committing it; but the Lord's Christ, the glorious Son of the everlasting Father, became a man and suffered in his own proper person the curse which was due to the sons of men, so that, by a vicarious offering God, having been just in punishing sin, could extend his bounteous mercy towards those who believe in the Substitute.

But, you inquire, how was Jesus Christ a curse? The answer is that 'He was *made* a curse.' Christ was no curse in himself. In his person he was spotlessly innocent, and nothing of sin could belong personally to him. In him was no sin. God 'made him who knew no sin to be sin for us' (*2 Cor.* 5:21). There must never be supposed to be any degree of blameworthiness or censure in the person or character of Christ as he stands as an individual. He is in that respect without spot or wrinkle, the immaculate Lamb of God's Passover. Nor was Christ made a curse out of necessity. There was no necessity for him ever to suffer the curse; no necessity except that which his own loving pledge created. His own intrinsic holiness kept him from sin, and that same holiness kept him from the curse. He was made sin *for us*, not on his own account, not with any view to himself, but wholly because he loved us and chose to put himself in the place which we ought to have occupied. He was made a curse for us, not out of any personal desert or out of any personal necessity, but because he had voluntarily undertaken to be the covenant head of his people, and to be their representative, and as their representative, to bear the curse which was due to them.

I want to be very clear here, because very strong expressions have been used by those who hold the great truth which I am endeavouring to preach; strong expressions which have conveyed the truth they meant to convey, but also a great deal more. Martin Luther prized the Epistle to the Galatians so much that he called it his his Catherine von Bora (that was the name of his beloved wife, and he gave this book the name of the dearest one he knew). In his book on that epistle he says plainly, but be assured he did not mean what he said to be literally understood, that, 'Jesus Christ was the greatest sinner that ever lived; that all the sins of man were so laid upon Christ that he became all the thieves, and murderers, and adulterers that ever were, in one.' Now he meant this: that God treated Christ as if he had been a great sinner; as if he had been all the sinners in the world in one; and such language teaches that truth very plainly. But Luther-like in his boisterousness, he overshoots his mark, and leaves room for the censure that he has almost spoken blasphemy against the blessed person of our Lord. Now, Christ never was and never could be a sinner; and in his person and in his character, in himself considered, he never could be anything but well beloved of God, and blessed forever and well pleasing in Jehovah's sight; so that when we say today that he was a curse, we must lay stress on those words, 'he was *made* a curse'—constituted a curse, set as a curse; and then again we must emphasize those other words, *for us*—not on his own account at all; but entirely out of love to us, that we might be redeemed; he stood in the sinner's place and was reckoned to be a sinner, and treated as a sinner and made a curse for us.

How was Christ made a curse? In the first place, he was made a curse because all the sins of his people were actually laid on him. 'He made him to be sin for us'; and let me quote from Isaiah, 'The Lord has laid on him the iniquity of us all'; and yet another statement from the same prophet, 'He shall bear their iniquities.' The sins of God's people were lifted from off them and imputed to Christ, and their sins were looked upon as if Christ had committed them. He was regarded as if he had been the sinner; he actually and in very deed stood in the sinner's place. Next to the imputation of sin came the curse of sin. The law, looking for sin to punish, with its quick eye detected sin laid upon Christ and, as it must curse sin wherever it was found, it cursed the sin as it was laid on Christ. So Christ was made a curse.

Wonderful and awful words, but, as they are scriptural words, we must receive them. Sin being on Christ, the curse came on Christ, and in consequence, our Lord felt an unutterable horror of soul. Surely it was that horror which made him sweat great drops of blood when he saw and felt that God was beginning to treat him as if he had been a sinner. The holy soul of Christ shrank with deepest agony from the slightest contact with sin. So pure and perfect was our Lord, that never an evil thought had crossed his mind, nor had his soul been stained by the glances of evil, and yet he stood in God's sight a sinner and therefore a solemn horror fell upon his soul. Then he began to be made a curse for us, nor did he cease till he had suffered all the penalty which was due on our account.

We have been accustomed to divide the penalty into two parts, the penalty of loss and the penalty of actual suffering. Christ endured both of these. It was due to sinners that they should lose God's favour and presence, and therefore Jesus cried, 'My God, my God, why hast thou forsaken me?' It was due to sinners that they should lose all personal comfort; Christ was deprived of every consolation, and even the last rag of clothing was torn from him and he was left, like Adam, naked and forlorn. It was necessary that the soul should lose everything that could sustain it, and so Christ lost every comfortable thing; he looked and there was no man to pity or help; he was made to cry, 'But I am a worm and no man; a reproach of men, and despised of the people' (*Ps.* 22:6). As for the second part of the punishment—namely, an actual infliction of suffering—our Lord endured this also to the extreme, as the evangelists clearly show. You have often read the story of his bodily sufferings; take care that you never depreciate them. There was an amount of physical pain endured by our Saviour which his body could never have borne unless it had been sustained and strengthened by union with his Godhead; yet the sufferings of his soul were the soul of his sufferings. That soul of his endured a torment equivalent to hell itself. The punishment that was due to the wicked was that of hell, and though Christ did not suffer hell, he suffered an equivalent for it; and now, can your minds conceive what that must have been? It was an anguish never to be measured, an agony never to be comprehended. It is to God, and God alone that his griefs were fully known. The Greek liturgy puts it well, 'Thine unknown sufferings', for they must forever remain beyond human imagination.

The consequences are that he has redeemed us from the curse of the law. Those for whom Christ died are forever free from the curse of the law; for when the law comes to curse a man who believes in Christ, he says, 'What have I to do with you, O law? You say, "I will curse you", but I reply, "You have cursed Christ instead of me. Can you curse twice for one offence?"' And the law is silenced! God's law having received all it can demand is not so unrighteous as to demand anything more. All that God can demand of a believing sinner, Christ has already paid, and there is no voice in earth or heaven that can accuse a soul that believes in Jesus after that. You were in debt, but a friend paid your debt; no writ can be served on you. It does not matter that *you* did not pay it, it is paid, and you have the receipt. That is sufficient in any fair court. So all the penalty that was due to us has been borne by Christ. It is true I have not borne it; I have not been to hell and suffered the full wrath of God, but Christ has suffered that wrath for me, and I am as clear as if I had paid the debt to God and suffered his wrath. Here is a glorious bottom to rest upon! Here is a rock upon which to lay the foundation of eternal comfort! Let a man get to this truth: my Lord outside the city's gate bled for me as my surety, and on the cross discharged my debt. Why then, great God, I no longer fear your thunder. How can you condemn me now? You have exhausted the quiver of your wrath; every arrow has already been used against my Lord, and I am in him clear and clean, absolved and delivered, as if I had never sinned.

'He hath redeemed us,' says the text. How often I have heard certain gentry of the modern school of theology sneer at the atonement, because they charge us with the notion of its being a sort of business transaction, or what they choose to call 'the mercantile view of it'. I do not hesitate to say that the mercantile metaphor rightly expresses God's view of redemption, for we find it so in Scripture; the atonement is a ransom—that is to say, a price paid; and in the present case the original word is more than usually expressive; it is a payment for, a price instead of. Jesus in his sufferings performed what may be forcibly and fitly described as the payment of a ransom, the giving to justice a *quid pro quo* for what was due on our behalf for our sins. Christ suffered what we ought to have suffered. The sins that were ours were made his; he stood as a sinner in God's sight; though not a sinner in himself, he was punished as a sinner, and died as a sinner upon the tree of the curse.

You have only to trust Christ, and you shall live. Whoever, or whatever, or wherever you are, even though you lie at hell's dark door to despair and die, the message comes to you: 'God hath made Christ to be a propitiation for sin. He made him to be sin for us who knew no sin, that we might be made the righteousness of God in him.' Christ has delivered us from the curse of the law, being made a curse for us. He who believes no longer has a curse upon him. He may have been an adulterer, a swearer, a drunkard, a murderer; but the moment he believes, God sees none of those sins in him. He sees him as an innocent man, and regards his sins as having been laid on the Redeemer, and punished in Jesus as he died on the tree. If you believe in Christ, though you are one of the most damnable wretches who ever polluted the earth, you shall not have a sin remaining on you after believing. God will look at you as pure; even Omniscience shall not detect a sin in you, for your sin shall be put on the scapegoat, even Christ, and carried away into forgetfulness.

Put away your accursed and idolatrous dependence upon yourself; Christ has finished salvation-work, altogether finished it. Do not hold your rags in competition with his fair white linen: Christ has borne the curse; do not bring your pitiful penances, and your tears all full of filth, to mingle with the precious fountain flowing with his blood. Lay down what is your own, and come and take what is Christ's. Put away now everything that you have thought of being or doing by way of winning acceptance with God; humble yourselves, and take Jesus Christ to be the Alpha and Omega, the first and last, the beginning and end of your salvation. If you do this, not only will you be saved, but you are saved. Rest, O weary one, for your sins are forgiven; rise, you lame man, lame through want of faith, for your transgression is covered; rise from the dead, you corrupt one, rise, like Lazarus from the tomb, for Jesus calls you! Believe and live.

10

Seeking

My main intention, to which I have set my whole soul, is to deal with those mourners who are seeking Christ, but until now have sought him in vain. Convinced of sin, awakened and alarmed, these unhappy ones wait for a long time outside the gate of mercy, shivering in the cold, pining to enter in to the banquet which invites them, but declining to pass through the gate which stands wide open for them. Tremblingly, they refuse to enter within mercy's open door, although infinite love itself cries to them, 'Come, and welcome: enter, and be blessed.' It is a most surprising thing that there should be in this world persons who have the richest consolation near to hand, and persistently refuse to take it. It seems so unnatural, that, if we had not been convinced by abundant observation, we should think it impossible that any miserable soul should refuse to be comforted. Does the ox refuse its fodder? Will the lion turn from his meat, or the eagle loathe its nest? The refusal of consolation is even more strange because the most admirable comfort is within reach. Sin can be forgiven; sin has been forgiven; Christ has made an atonement for it. God is graciously willing to accept any sinner who comes to him confessing his transgressions, and trusting in the blood of the Lord Jesus. God waits to be gracious, he is not hard nor harsh; he is full of mercy; he delights to pardon the penitent, and is never more revealed in the glory of his God-head than when he is accepting the unworthy through the righteousness of Jesus Christ. There is so much comfort in the Word of God that it is as easy to set the limits of space as it is to measure the grace revealed there. You may seek to comprehend all the sweetness of divine love, but you cannot, for it passes knowledge. The abounding goodness of God made manifest in Jesus Christ is like the vast expanse of the ocean. It is extraordinary, then, that men refuse to receive what is so lavishly provided.

It is said that, some years ago, a vessel sailing on the northern coast of the South American continent was observed to make signals of distress. When hailed by another vessel, they reported themselves as 'Dying for water!' 'Dip it up, then,' was the response; 'you are in the mouth of the Amazon river.' There was fresh water all around them, they had nothing to do but to dip it up, and yet they were dying of thirst, because they thought themselves to be surrounded by the salt sea. How often are men ignorant of their mercies! How sad that they should perish for lack of knowledge!

But suppose, after the sailors had received the joyful information, they had still refused to draw up the water which was in boundless plenty all around them, would it not have been a marvel? Would you not at once conclude that madness had taken hold of the captain and his crew? Yet this is the sort of madness of many who hear the gospel. They know that there is mercy provided for sinners; that unless the Holy Spirit interferes they will perish, not through ignorance, but because, for some reason or other, like the Jews of old, they judge themselves 'unworthy of everlasting life'; yet they still exclude themselves from the gospel, refusing to be comforted. This is even more remarkable because the comfort provided is so safe. If there were suspicions that the comforts of the gospel would prove delusive, that they would only foster presumption and so destroy the soul, men would be wise to retreat as if from a cup of poison. But many have satisfied themselves at this life-giving stream; not one has been injured, but all who have drunk have been eternally blessed.

Why, then, does the thirsty soul hesitate, while the river, clear as crystal, flows at his feet? Moreover, *the comfort of the gospel is entirely suitable*, it is *fully adapted* to the sinful, the weak, and the broken-hearted, adapted to those who are crushed by their need of mercy, and adapted equally as much to those who are least aware of their need of it. The gospel bears a balm in its hand suited to the sinner in his worst state, when he has nothing good about him, and nothing within him which can possibly be a ground of hope. Does the gospel not declare that Christ died for the ungodly? Is it not a faithful saying and worthy of all acceptation that Christ Jesus came into the world to save sinners, of whom, said the apostle, 'I am chief'? Is the gospel not intended even for those who are dead in sin? Do we not read words such as these, 'God, who is rich in mercy, for his great love wherewith he loved us, even when we were dead in sins, hath quickened us together with Christ (by grace ye are saved)'? Are the invitations of the gospel, so far as we can judge, not the kindest, tenderest, and most attractive that could be penned and addressed to the worst emergency in which a sinner can be placed? 'Ho, everyone that thirsteth, come ye to the waters, and he that hath no money; come ye, buy, and eat; yea, come, buy wine and milk without money and without price' (*Isa.* 55:1). 'Let the wicked forsake his way, and the unrighteous man his thoughts; and let him return unto the Lord, and he will have mercy upon him; and to our God, for he will abundantly pardon' (*Isa.* 55:7). No qualifying adjectives are used to set forth a degree of goodness in the person invited, but the wicked are asked to come, and the unrighteous are commanded to turn to God. The invitation deals with base, naked, unimproved sinnership. Grace seeks for misery, unworthiness, guilt, helplessness, and nothing else. Not because we are good, but because the Lord is gracious, we are bidden to believe in the infinite mercy of God in Christ Jesus, and so to receive comfort. It is strange that where consolation

[56]

is so plentiful—where comfort is so safe, where the heart-cheer is so suitable—thousands of souls should be found who refuse to be comforted.

This fact grows still more remarkable because these persons greatly need comfort, and from what they say, and I trust also from what they feel, you might infer that comfort was the very thing they would clutch at, as a drowning man does at a rope. Why, they scarcely sleep at night by reason of their fears. By day their faces betray the sorrow which, like a tumultuous sea, rages within them. They can scarcely speak a cheerful sentence. They make their household miserable; the infection of their sorrow is caught by others. You would think that the very moment the word 'hope' was whispered in their ears, they would leap towards it at once; but it is not so. You may put the gospel into whatever shape you please, and yet these poor souls who need your pity, though, I fear, they must also have your blame, refuse to be comforted. Though food is placed before them, their soul abhors all kinds of meat, and they draw near to the gates of death; indeed, you may even put the heavenly cordial into their mouths, but they will not receive the spiritual nutrition; they pine in hunger rather than take what divine love provides.

When the dove was weary, she remembered the ark and flew into Noah's hand at once; these people are weary and they know the ark, but they will not fly to it. When an Israelite had killed, inadvertently, his fellow, he knew the city of refuge, he feared the avenger of blood, and he fled along the road to the place of safety. These sinners know the refuge, and every Sabbath we set up the signposts along the road, but still they do not come to find salvation. The destitute waifs and strays of the streets of London find out the night-refuge and ask for shelter; they cluster round our workhouse doors like sparrows under the eaves of a building on a rainy day; they piteously crave for lodging and a crust of bread; yet crowds of poor benighted spirits, when the house of mercy is lit up and the invitation is plainly written in bold letters, 'Whosoever will, let him turn in hither', will not come.

For many sinners, their refusal to be comforted arises from *bodily and mental disease*. It is in vain to ply with scriptural arguments those who are in more urgent need of healing medicine, or a generous diet. There is so close a connection between the sphere of the physician and the divine that they do well to hunt in couples when chasing the delusions of morbid humanity; and I am persuaded that there are many cases in which the minister's presence is of little use until the physician has first wisely discharged his part.

In some people, the monstrous refusal is suggested by a *proud dislike to the plan of salvation*. They would be comforted, but may they not do something to earn eternal life? May they not at least contribute a feeling or emotion? May they not prepare themselves for Christ? Must salvation be all gratis? Must they be received into the house of mercy as paupers? Must they come with no other cry but, 'God be merciful to me a sinner'? Must it come to this—to be stripped, to have every rag of one's own righteousness torn away, even the righteousness of feeling as well as the righteousness of doing? Must the whole head be confessedly sick, and the whole heart faint, and the man lie before Jesus as utterly undone and ruined, to take everything from the hand of the crucified Saviour? Ah then, says flesh and blood, I will not have it. The banner of self is held up by a giant standard-bearer; it floats on long after the battle has been lost. But what folly! For the sake of indulging a foolish dignity we will not be comforted. Down with you and your dignity! I beseech you, bow down now before the feet of Jesus and kiss the feet which were nailed for your sins.

In others it is not pride, but an unholy resolve to retain some favourite sin. In most cases when the Christian minister tries to heal a wound that has long been bleeding, he probes

[58]

and probes again with his lancet, wondering why the wound will not heal. It seems to him that all the circumstances augur a successful healing of the wound. He cannot imagine why it still continues to bleed, but at last he finds out the secret: 'Ah, here I have it; here is an extraneous substance which continually frets and aggravates the wounds; it cannot heal while this grit of sin lies within it.' In some cases we have found out that the sorrowing person still indulged in a secret vice, or kept the society of the ungodly, or was undutiful to parents, or unforgiving, or slothful, or practised that hideous sin, secret drunkenness. In such a case, if the man resolves, 'I will not give up this sin', is it any wonder he is not comforted? Would it not be an awful thing if he were? When a man carries a corroding substance within his soul, if his wound is filmed over, an internal disease will come of it and prove deadly. Confess to Jesus, who will forgive all your foolishness and accept you, so that you shall refuse to be comforted no longer.

Some refuse to be comforted because of an obstinate determination only to be comforted in a way of their own selecting. They have read the life of a certain good man who was saved with a particular kind of experience. 'Now', they say, 'if I feel like that man, then I shall conclude I am saved.' Many have hit upon the experience in *Grace Abounding*; they have said, 'Now I must be brought just as John Bunyan was, or else I will not believe.' Another has said, 'I must tread the path which John Newton trod—my feet must be placed in the very marks where his feet went down, or else I cannot believe in Jesus Christ.' But what reason have you for expecting that God will yield to your self-will, and what justification have you for prescribing to the Great Physician the methods of his cure? Oh, if he brings me to heaven I will bless him, even though he may conduct me there by the gates of hell. If I am brought to see the King in his beauty, in the land which is very far off, it shall not trouble my heart by what method of experience he brought me there. Come, lay aside this foolish choosing of yours, and say, 'Lord, have mercy on me, enable me to trust your dear Son, and my whims and my fancies will be given up.'

I fear, in many, there is another reason for refusing to be comforted—namely, a dishonouring unbelief in the love and goodness and truthfulness of God. They do not believe God to be gracious; they think him a tyrant, or if not quite that, One so stern that a sinner needed to plead and beg for a long time before the heart of God will be touched. Oh, but you do not know my God! What is he? He is love. I tell you he wants no persuading to have mercy, any more than the sun needs to be persuaded to shine, or a fountain to pour out its streams. It is the nature of God to be gracious. He is never so godlike as when he is bestowing mercy. 'Judgment is his strange work'; it is his left-handed work; but mercy, the last manifested of his attributes, is his Benjamin, the child of his right hand, he delights to exercise it. Is it not written that, 'He delighteth in mercy'? Alas! alas! that God should be slandered by those to whom he speaks so lovingly! 'As I live, saith the Lord,' here he takes an oath, and will you not believe him? 'As I live, saith the Lord God, I have no pleasure in the death of the wicked; but that the wicked turn from his way and live. Turn ye, turn ye! . . . for why will ye die, O house of Israel?' (*Ezek.* 33:11). He even seems to turn beggar to his own creatures, and to plead with them to come to him. He yearns for their salvation as he cries, 'How shall I give thee up, Ephraim? how shall I deliver thee, Israel? how shall I make thee as Admah? how shall I set thee as Zeboim? Mine heart is turned within me, my repentings are kindled together. I will not execute the fierceness of mine anger, I will not return to destroy Ephraim, for I am God, and not man' (*Hos.* 11:8–9). Oh, do not, I beseech you, be unbelieving any longer, but believe God's word and oath, and accept the comfort which he freely offers to you in the words of his gospel!

Some however, have refused comfort so long, that they have grown into *the habit of despair*. Ah, it is a dangerous habit, and trembles on the brink of hell. Every moment in which it is indulged a man grows inured to it. It is like the cold of the frigid zone, which benumbs the traveller after a while, till he feels nothing and drops into slumber, and from that into death. Some have despaired and despaired until they had reason for despair, and until despair brought them into hell. Despair has hardened some men's hearts till they have been ready to commit sins which hope would have rendered impossible to them. Beware of nursing despondency. Does it creep upon you through unbelief? Oh, shake it off, if possible! Cry to the Holy Spirit, the Comforter, to loose you from this snare of the fowler; for, depend upon it, doubting God is a net of Satan, and blessed is he who escapes its toils. Believing in God strengthens the soul and brings us both holiness and happiness, but distrusting, and suspecting, and surmising, and fearing, hardens the heart, and renders us less likely ever to come to God. Beware of despair; and may you, if you have fallen into this evil habit, be snatched from it as the brand from the burning fire, and delivered by the Lord, who looses his prisoner.

11

How Luther Sought and Found

Luther's voice through four hundred years still sounds in the
ears of men, and quickens our pulses like the beat of a drum
in martial music: he lives because he was a man of faith.

I would like to illustrate this by describing certain inci-
dents of Luther's life. Gospel light broke by slow degrees
upon the reformer's life. It was in the monastery that, in
turning over the old Bible that was chained to a pillar, he
came upon this passage: 'The just shall live by his faith.' This
heavenly sentence stuck to him; but he hardly understood all
its significance. He could not, however, find peace in his
religious profession and monastic habits. Knowing no better, he persevered in so many penances and such arduous
mortifications that sometimes he was found fainting through
exhaustion. He brought himself to death's door. He must
make a journey to Rome, for in Rome there is a fresh church
for every day, and you may be sure to win the pardon of sins
and all sorts of benedictions in these holy shrines. He
dreamed of entering a city of holiness; but he found it to be
a haunt of hypocrites and a den of iniquity. To his horror he
heard men say that if there was a hell, Rome was built on top
of it, for it was the nearest approach to it that could be found
in this world; but still he believed in its Pope and he went on
with his penances, seeking rest but finding none.

One day he was climbing upon his knees the Scala Sancta,
which still stands in Rome. I have stood amazed at the bottom of the staircase to see poor creatures go up and down on

their knees in the belief that it is the very staircase that our Lord descended when he left Pilate's house, and certain steps are said to be marked with drops of blood; these the poor souls kiss most devoutly. Well, Luther was crawling up these steps one day, when that same text which he had met with before in the monastery sounded like a clap of thunder in his ears, 'The just shall live by his faith.' He rose from his prostration, and went down the steps never to grovel upon them again. At that moment the Lord brought him a full deliverance from superstition, and he saw that he was to live not by priests, nor priestcraft, nor penances, nor by anything that he could do, but that he must live by his faith.

No sooner did he believe this than he began to live, in the sense of being active. Tetzel was going about all over Germany selling the forgiveness of sins for so much ready cash. No matter what your offence, as soon as your money touched the bottom of the box your sins were gone. Luther heard of this, grew indignant, and exclaimed, 'I will make a hole in his drum,' which assuredly he did, and in several other drums. The nailing up of his Theses on the church door was a sure way of silencing the indulgence music. Luther proclaimed pardon of sin by faith in Christ without money and without price, and the pope's indulgences were soon objects of derision. Luther lived by his faith, and therefore he who otherwise might have been quiet, denounced error as furiously as a lion roars upon his prey. The faith that was in him filled him with intense life, and he plunged into war with the enemy.

After a while they summoned him to Augsburg, and to Augsburg he went, though his friends advised him not to go. They summoned him, as a heretic, to answer for himself at the Diet of Worms, and everybody urged him to stay away, for he would be sure to be burned; but he felt it necessary that the testimony should be borne, and so in a wagon he went, from village to village and town to town, preaching as he went, the poor people coming out to shake hands with the man who was

[63]

standing up for Christ and the gospel at the risk of his life. You remember how he stood before that august assembly, and though he knew, as far as human power went, that his defence would cost him his life, for he would probably be committed to the flames like John Huss, yet he stood for the Lord his God. That day in the German Diet, Luther did a work for which ten thousand times ten thousand mothers' children have blessed his name, and blessed yet more the name of the Lord his God.

To put him out of harm's way for a while a prudent friend took him prisoner, and kept him out of the strife in the castle of Wartburg. There he had a good time of it, resting, studying, translating, making music, and preparing himself for the future which was to be so eventful. He did all that a man can do who is outside of the fray; but 'the just shall live by his faith', and Luther could not be buried alive in ease, he had to be getting on with his life-work.

He sent word to his friends that he would soon be with them, and he then appeared at Wittenberg. The prince meant to have kept him in retirement somewhat longer; and when the Elector feared that he could not protect him, Luther wrote: 'I come under far higher protection than yours; nay, I hold that I am more likely to protect your Grace than your Grace to protect me. He who has the strongest faith is the best protector.' Luther had learned to be independent of all men, for he cast himself upon his God. He had all the world against him, and yet he lived happily—if the Pope excommunicated him, he burned the bull; if the Emperor threatened him, he rejoiced because he remembered the word of the Lord: 'The kings of the earth set themselves, and the rulers take counsel together. . . . He that sitteth in the heavens shall laugh' (*Ps.* 2:2, 4). When they said to him, 'Where will you find shelter if the Elector does not protect you?' he answered, 'Under the broad shield of God.'

Luther could not be still; he had to speak, and write, and

thunder; and oh, with what confidence he spoke! Doubts about God and Scripture he abhorred. Melanchthon says he was not dogmatical. I rather differ from Melanchthon there, and reckon Luther to be the chief of dogmatics. He called Melanchthon the 'soft treader', and I wonder what we should have done if Luther had been Melanchthon, and had trodden softly, too. The times needed a firmly assured leader, and faith made Luther all that for years, notwithstanding his many sorrows and infirmities. He was a Titan, a giant, a man of splendid mental calibre and strong physique: and yet his main life and force lay in his faith. He suffered greatly in exercises of the mind and through diseases of body, and these might well have occasioned a display of weakness; but that weakness did not appear; for when he believed, he was as sure of what he believed as of his own existence, and therefore he was strong. If every angel in heaven had passed before him and each one had assured him of the truth of God he would not have thanked them for their testimony, for he believed God without the witness of either angels or men: he thought the word of divine testimony more sure than anything that seraphim could say.

This man was forced to live by his faith, for he was a man of stormy soul and only faith could speak peace to him. Those stirring excitements of his brought on him afterwards fearful depressions of spirit, and then he needed faith in God. If you read a spiritual life of him you will find that it was hard work sometimes for him to keep his soul alive. Being a man of like passions with us, and full of imperfections, he was at times as despondent and despairing as the weakest among us; and the swelling grief within him threatened to burst his mighty heart. But both he and John Calvin frequently sighed for the rest of heaven, for they did not love the strife in which they lived, but would have been glad peacefully to feed the flock of God on earth and then to enter into rest. These men dwelt with God in holy boldness of believing prayer, or they could not have lived at all.

Luther's faith laid hold upon the cross of our Lord, and would not be stirred from it. He believed in the forgiveness of sins, and could not afford to doubt it. He cast anchor upon Holy Scripture, and rejected all the inventions of clerics and all the traditions of the fathers. He was assured of the truth of the gospel, and never doubted that it would prevail, though earth and hell were leagued against it. When he came to die his old enemy assailed him fiercely, but when they asked him if he held the same faith his 'Yes' was positive enough. They need not have asked him, they should have been sure of that. And now today the truth proclaimed by Luther continues to be preached, and will be till our Lord himself shall come. Then the holy city will need no candle, nor the light of the sun, because the Lord himself will be the light of his people; but till then we must shine with gospel light to our utmost.

12

Saved through Faith

The way of salvation has always been the same. No man has
ever been saved by his good works. The way by which the
just have lived has always been the way of faith. There has
not been the slightest advance upon this truth; it is established and settled, ever the same, like the God who uttered it.
At all times, and everywhere, the gospel is and must forever
be the same. 'Jesus Christ the same yesterday, and today, and
for ever' (*Heb.* 13:8). We read of 'the gospel' as one; never of
two or three gospels. Heaven and earth shall pass away, but
Christ's Word shall never pass away.

It is also noteworthy not only that this truth should be so
old, and should continue so unchanged, but that it should
possess such vitality. This one sentence, 'The just shall live
by his faith', produced the Reformation. Out of this one line,
as from the opening of one of the apocalyptic seals, came
forth all that sounding of gospel trumpets, and all that singing of gospel songs, which sounded like the noise of many
waters in the world. This one seed, forgotten and hidden
away in the dark medieval times, was brought out, dropped
into the human heart, and made to grow by the Spirit of God
so that it produced great results. The least bit of truth,
thrown anywhere, will live! Certain plants are so full of vitality that if you only take a fragment of a leaf and place it on the
soil, the leaf will take root and grow. It is utterly impossible
that such vegetation should become extinct; and so it is with
the truth of God—it is living and incorruptible, and therefore

there is no destroying it. As long as one Bible remains, the religion of free grace will live; indeed, if they could burn all printed Scriptures, as long as there remained a child who remembered a single text of the Word, the truth would rise again. Even in the ashes of truth the fire is still living, and when the breath of the Lord blows upon it, the flame will burst forth gloriously.

In the Old Testament we are told that Abraham 'believed in the Lord; and he counted it to him for righteousness' (*Gen.* 15:6). This is the universal plan of justification. Faith lays hold upon the righteousness of God, by accepting God's plan of justifying sinners through the sacrifice of Jesus Christ, and thus makes the sinner righteous. Faith accepts and appropriates for itself the whole system of divine righteousness which is unfolded in the person and work of the Lord Jesus. Faith rejoices to see him coming into the world in our nature and in that nature obeying the law in every jot and tittle, though not himself under that law until he chose to put himself there on our behalf; faith is further pleased when it sees the Lord, who had come under the law, offering up himself as a perfect atonement and making a complete vindication of divine justice by his sufferings and death.

Faith lays hold upon the person, life and death of the Lord Jesus as its sole hope, and in the righteousness of Christ it arrays itself. It cries, 'The chastisement of my peace was upon him, and by his stripes I am healed.' Now, the man who believes in God's method of making men righteous through the righteousness of Jesus, and accepts Jesus and leans upon him is a just man. He who makes the life and death of God's great propitiation his sole reliance and confidence is justified in the sight of God, and is written down among the just by the Lord himself. His faith is imputed to him for righteousness because his faith grasps the righteousness of God in Christ Jesus. 'All that believe are justified from all things, from which ye could not be justified by the law of Moses' (*Acts*

13:39). This is the testimony of the inspired Word, and who shall deny it?

But the believer is also just in another sense, which the outside world appreciates more, though it is no more valuable than the former. The man who believes in God becomes by that faith moved to everything that is right, and good, and true. His faith in God rectifies his mind, and makes him just. In judgment, in desire, in aspiration, in heart, he is just. His sin has been forgiven him freely and now, in the hour of temptation, he cries, 'How then can I do this great wickedness, and sin against God?' He believes in the blood-shedding which God has provided for the cleansing of sin, and, being washed in that blood, he cannot choose to defile himself again.

The love of Christ constrains him to seek after whatever is true, and right, and good, and loving, and honourable in the sight of God. Having received by faith the privilege of adoption, he strives to live as a child of God. Having obtained by faith a new life, he walks in the newness of life. 'Immortal principles forbid the child of God to sin.' If any man lives in sin and loves it, he does not have the faith of God's elect; for true faith purifies the soul. The faith which is worked out in us by the Holy Spirit is the greatest sin-killer under heaven. By the grace of God it affects the inmost heart, changes the desires and the affections, and makes the man a new creature in Christ Jesus. If there are on earth any who can truly be called just, they are those who are made so by faith in God through Jesus Christ our Lord. Indeed, no other men are 'just' except those to whom the holy God gives the title, and these live by faith. Faith trusts God, and therefore loves him, and therefore obeys him, and therefore grows like him. It is the root of holiness, the spring of righteousness, the life of the just.

God is so true that to doubt him is an injustice: and he who does the Lord such an injustice is not a just man. A just man must first be just with the greatest of all beings. It would be idle for him to be just to his fellow creatures only, if he did a wilful injustice to God. In fact, he would be unworthy of the name of just. Faith is what the Lord justly deserves to receive from his creatures: it is his due that we believe in what he says, and specially in reference to the gospel. When the great love of God in Christ Jesus is plainly expressed, it will be believed by the pure in heart. If the great love of Christ in dying for us is fully understood, it must be believed by every honest mind. To doubt the witness of God concerning his Son is to do the sorest injustice to infinite love. He who does not believe has rejected God's witness to the unspeakable gift and rejected that which deserves man's adoring gratitude, since it alone can satisfy the justice of God and give peace to the conscience of man. A truly just man must, in order to be completely just, believe in God, and in all that he has revealed.

Some dream that this matter of justness only concerns the outer life, and does not touch man's belief. I say this is not so; righteousness concerns the inner parts of a man, the central region of his manhood; and truly just men desire to be made clean in the secret parts, and in the hidden parts they would know wisdom. Is it not so? We hear it continually asserted that the understanding and the belief constitute a province exempt from the jurisdiction of God. Is it indeed true that I may believe what I like without being accountable to God for my belief? No single part of our manhood is beyond the range of the divine law. Our whole capacity as men lies under the sovereignty of him who created us, and we are bound as much to believe rightly as we are bound to act rightly; in fact, our actions and our thoughts are so intertwined and entangled that it is impossible to divide one from the other. To say that the rightness of the outward life suffices is to argue contrary to the whole tenor of the Word of God. I am bound as much to serve God with my mind as with my heart. I am bound as much to believe what God reveals as I am to do what God enjoins.

'The just shall live *by faith*.' This sentence savours of the strait gate which stands at the head of the way—the narrow way which leads into eternal life. At one blow this ends all claims of righteousness apart from one mode of life. The best men in the world can only live by faith, there is no other way of being just in the sight of God. We cannot live in righteousness by self. If we are going to trust ourselves, or anything that comes from ourselves, we have not known the life of God according to the teaching of Holy Writ. You must abandon all confidence in everything that you are or hope to be. You must tear off the leprous garment of legal righteousness, and part with self in any and every form. Self-reliance as to the things of religion will be found to be self-destruction; you must rest in God as he is revealed in his Son Jesus Christ, and there alone.

The just shall live by faith; but those who look to the works of the law are under the curse, and cannot live before God. The same is also true of those who endeavour to live by sense or feeling. They judge God by what they see: if he is bountiful to them in providence, he is a good God; if they are poor, they have nothing good to say of him, for they measure him by what they feel, and taste, and see. If God works steadily to a purpose, and they can see his purpose, they commend his wisdom; but when they either cannot see the purpose, or cannot understand the way by which the Lord is working to attain it, immediately they judge him to be unwise. Living by sense turns out to be a senseless mode of life, bringing death to all comfort and hope.

Too many say, 'I am my own guide, I shall make doctrines for myself, and I shall shift them and shape them according to my own devices.' This is death to the spirit. To be abreast of the times is to be an enemy to God. The way of life is to believe what God has taught, especially to believe in him whom God has set forth to be a propitiation for sin; for that is making God to be everything and ourselves nothing. Resting on an infallible revelation and trusting in an omnipotent Redeemer, we have rest and peace; but on the other unsettled principle we become wandering stars, for whom is appointed the blackness of darkness forever. By faith the soul can live; in all other ways we have a name to live and are dead.

The same is equally true of fancy. We often meet with a fanciful religion in which people trust impulses, dreams, noises and mystic things which they imagine they have seen: fiddle-faddle all of it, and yet they are quite wrapped up in it. I pray that you may cast out this chaffy stuff, for there is no food for the spirit in it. The life of my soul lies not in what I think, or what I fancy, or what I imagine, or what I enjoy of fine feeling, but only in that which faith apprehends to be the Word of God. We live before God by trusting a promise, depending on a person, accepting a sacrifice, wearing a righteousness, and surrendering ourselves up to God—Father, Son, and Holy Spirit. Implicit trust in Jesus, our Lord, is the way of life, and every other way leads to death. Let those who call this statement narrow or intolerant say what they please; it will be just as true when they have execrated it as it is now.

Much is comprehended in the saying, 'The just shall live by his faith.' It does not say what part of his life hangs on his believing, or what phase of his life best proves his believing: it comprehends the beginning, continuance, increase, and perfecting of spiritual life as being all by faith. The moment a man believes, he begins to live in the sight of God: he trusts his God, he accepts God's revelation of himself, he confides, reposes, leans upon his Saviour, and that moment he becomes a spiritually living man, quickened with spiritual life by God the Holy Spirit. All his existence before that belief was only a form of death: when he comes to trust in God he enters upon eternal life, and is born from above.

Yes, but that is not all, nor even half of it; for if that man is to continue living before God, if he is to hold on his way in holiness, his perseverance must be the result of continued faith. The faith which saves is not one single act done and ended on a certain day: it is an act continued and persevered in throughout the entire life of a man. The just not only commences to live by his faith, but he continues to live by his faith: he does not begin in the spirit and end in the flesh, nor go so far by grace, and the rest of the way by the works of the law. 'The just shall live by faith,' says the text in the Hebrews, 'but if any man draw back, my soul shall have no pleasure in him. But we are not of them who draw back unto perdition; but of them that believe to the saving of the soul' (*Heb.* 10:38–39). Faith is essential all along; every day and all day, in all things. Our natural life begins by breathing, and it must be continued by breathing: what the breath is to the body, faith is to the soul.

13

May I Believe?

You know who Jesus is, and you believe him to be the Son of God, the Saviour of men. You are sure that 'he is able to save them to the uttermost that come unto God by him'. You have no doubt about those eternal truths which surround his Godhead, his birth, his life, his death, his resurrection, and his Second Advent. The doubt is concerning yourself personally—'If I may be a partaker of this salvation.' You feel quite certain that faith in Jesus Christ will save anyone—will save you if you exercise it. You have no doubt about the doctrine of justification by faith. You have learned it, and you have received it as a matter beyond all dispute, that he who believes in him has everlasting life; and you know that he who comes to him will not be cast out. You know the remedy, and believe in its efficacy; but then comes the doubt—may I be healed by it? At the back of your belief in faith hides the gloomy thought: 'May I believe? May I trust? I see the door is open: many are entering. May I? I see that there is washing from the worst of sins in the sacred fount. Many are being cleansed. May I wash and be clean?' Without formulating a doubt so as to express it, it comes up in all sorts of ways, and robs you of all comfort, and, indeed, of all hope. When a sermon is preached it is like when someone sets a table out with all manner of dainties, and you look at it but do not feel that you have any right to sit down and begin eating. This is a wretched delusion. Its result will be deadly unless you are delivered from it. Like a rapacious monster it preys upon you. When you see the brooks flowing with their sparkling streams, and you are thirsty, do you think that you are not permitted to drink? If so, you are out of your mind; you talk and think like one bereft of reason. Yet many are in this state spiritually. This doubting your liberty to come to Jesus is a wretched business; it mars and spoils your reading and your hearing and your attempts to pray; and you will never get any comfort until this question has been answered in your heart once for all, 'May I?'

I defy you, if you read all the Old and New Testaments through, to put your finger upon a single verse in which God has said that you may not come and put your trust in Christ. Perhaps you will reply that you do not expect to read it in the Bible, but God may have said it somewhere where it is not recorded. Well, he says, 'I have not spoken in secret, in a dark place of the earth: I said not unto the seed of Jacob, Seek ye me in vain' (*Isa.* 45:19). Now, he has commanded you over and over again to seek his face, but he has never said that you shall seek his face in vain. Dismiss that thought. Again I return to what I have said: there is nothing in Scripture that refuses you permission to come and repose your soul once for all upon Christ. It is written, 'Whosoever will, let him take the water of life freely' (*Rev.* 22:17). Does that exclude you? It is written, 'Whosoever shall call upon the name of the Lord shall be saved' (*Rom.* 10:13). Does that shut you out? No, it includes you; it invites you; it encourages you. Nowhere in the Word of God is it written that you will be cast out if you come, or that Jesus Christ will not remove your burden of sin if you come and lay it at his feet.

A thousand passages of Scripture welcome you, but not one stands with a drawn sword to keep you back from the tree of life. Our heavenly Father sets his angels at the gates of his house to welcome all comers; but there are no dogs to bark at poor beggars nor notices that trespassers must beware. Come and be welcome.

Don't you think that the very nature of the Lord Jesus Christ should forbid your raising a doubt about your being permitted to come and touch his garment's hem? Surely, if anyone were to paint the Lord Jesus Christ as an ascetic, repelling with lofty pride the humbler folk who had never reached his dignity of consecration; if any were to paint him as a Pharisee driving off publicans and sinners, or as an iceberg of righteousness chilling the sinful, it would be a foul slander upon his divine character. If anyone were to say that Jesus Christ is exacting—that he will not receive to himself the guilty just as they are, but requires a great deal of them and will only welcome to himself those who are, like himself, good and true and excellent—that would not be truth, but the direct opposite of it. For the accusation that 'this man receiveth sinners, and eateth with them' was thrown in his face when he lived on earth; and what the prophet said of him was most certainly true: 'A bruised reed shall he not break, and the smoking flax shall he not quench' (*Isa.* 42:3).

Little children are wonderful judges of character; they know intuitively who is kind. And so are loving women. They do not go through the processes of reasoning, but they come to a conclusion very soon as to a man's personal character. Now, the children came and clambered on our Redeemer's knee, and the mothers brought their infants for his blessing. How can you dream that he will repel *you*? The women wept and beseeched him, and felt pity for those who refused him, so I am sure that he is not hard to move. Therefore I want you to feel sure of this—that there is nothing in the Saviour's character which can for a moment lead him to discard you and to drive you from his presence.

Those who know him best will say that it is impossible for him ever to refuse the poor and needy. A blind man could not cry to him without receiving sight, nor a hungry man look to him without being fed. He was touched with a feeling of our infirmities—the most gentle, and loving, and tender of all

[76]

who ever lived upon this earth. I beseech you, therefore, to take it for granted that you may come boldly to him without fear of a rebuff. If he has power to heal you when you touch him, rest assured that you may touch him. There is no question that you may believe; for Jesus is too loving to refuse you. It will give him joy to receive you. It is not possible that he should refuse you; it is not in his nature to spurn you from his presence.

Will you think, yet again, of the fullness of Christ's power to save, and make a little argument of it? Christ was so full of power to bless that the secret virtue even saturated his clothes. It overflowed his blessed person; it ran down to the skirts of his garments, even to that hem which every Jew wore around his dress—that fringe of blue. It went into that border so that when the woman simply touched the ravellings of his garment, virtue streamed into her (*Luke* 8:42–48). If the touch was a touch of faith, it did not matter where the contact was made. You often judge a man's willingness to help by the power that he has. When a person has little to give he is bound to be economical in his giving. He must look at every penny before he gives it, if he has so few pence to spare. But when a nobleman has no limit to his estate, you feel sure that he will freely give if his heart is generous and tender. The blessed Lord is so full of healing power that he cannot stop himself working healing miracles; and according to the goodness of his nature he is delighted to overflow, glad to communicate to those who come. You know that if a city is short of water, the corporation sends out an order that only so much may be used, and there is a restriction imposed upon public baths and factories, because there is a scarcity of the precious fluid. But if you go along the Thames when we have had a rainy season, you laugh at the notion of a short supply and economical rules. If a dog wants to drink from a river, nobody ever questions his right to do so. He comes down to the water and he laps, and, what is more, he runs right into it, regardless of those who may have to drink after him. Look at the cattle, how they stand knee-deep in the stream and drink, and drink again; and nobody ever says, as he goes up the Thames, that those poor London people will run short of water, for the dogs and the cattle are drinking it up before it gets down to London. No, it never enters our head to petition the owners of these dogs and cows to restrain them; for there is so much water that there must be liberty to everyone to drink to the full. Your question is, 'May I? May I?' I answer that question by saying this: there is nothing to forbid you; there is everything in the nature of Christ to encourage you; and there is so much mercy in him that you cannot think that he can have the slightest motive for withholding his infinite grace.

Moreover, suppose you come to Christ as this woman came, and touch the hem of his garment, you will not injure him. You ought to hesitate in gaining benefit for yourself if you would injure the person through whom you obtain that good. But you will not injure the Lord Jesus Christ. He perceived that virtue had gone out of him, but he did not perceive it by any pain he felt: I believe that he perceived it by the pleasure which it caused him. Something gave him unusual joy. A faith-touch had reached him through his clothes, and he rejoiced to respond by imparting healing virtue from himself.

You will not defile my Lord, O sinner, if you bring him all your sin. He will not have to die again to put away your fresh burden of transgression. He will not have to shed one drop of blood to atone for your multiplied sin: the one sacrifice on Calvary anticipated all possible guiltiness. If you will come just as you are, he will not have to leave heaven again, and be born again on earth, and live another sorrowful life in order to save you. He will not need to wear another crown of thorns, or bear another wound in his hands, or feet, or side. He has done all his atoning work: do you not remember his victorious cry—'It is finished'? You cannot injure him though all your injurious thoughts, words and speeches be laid upon him. You will not be robbing him of anything, though your faith-touch conveys life to you. He has such a fullness about him, that if all you poor sinners come at once, when you have taken away all the merit that you need there will be as much merit left as there was before. When you deal with the infinite you may divide and subtract, but you cannot diminish. If the whole race were washed in the infinite fountain of Jesus' merit, the infinite would still remain.

Others just like you have ventured to him, and there has not been a case in which they have been refused. I thought, like you, when I was a child, that the gospel was a very wonderful thing, and free to everybody but myself. I should not have wondered at all if my brother and sisters as well as my father and mother had been saved; but, somehow, I could not get a hold of it myself. It was a precious thing, as much out of my reach as the Queen's diamonds. So I thought. To many the gospel is like a tram-car in motion, and they cannot jump upon it. I thought surely everybody would be saved, but I should not; and yet, soon after I began to cry for mercy, I found it. My expectations of difficulty were all sweetly disappointed. I believed and found immediate rest to my soul. When I once understood that 'There was life for a look at the Crucified One,' I gave that look, and I found eternal life.

Nobody ever bears a different witness. I challenge the universe to produce a man who was chased from Christ's door, or forbidden to find in him a Saviour. I beg you, therefore, to observe that since others have come this way to life and peace, God has appointed it to be the common thoroughfare of grace. Poor guilty sinners, there is a sign set up, 'This way for sinners. This way for the guilty. This way for the hungry. This way for the thirsty. This way for the lost. Come to me, all you who labour and are heavy laden, and I will give you rest.' Why, surely, you need not say, 'If I may.' There is no room to say, 'If I may,' because, first of all, you are invited to come and accept Christ as your Saviour—invited over and over again in the Word of God. 'The Spirit and the bride say, Come. And let him that heareth say, Come. And let him that is athirst come. And whosoever will, let him take the water of life freely' (*Rev.* 22:17). 'Ho, every one that thirsteth, come ye to the waters, and he that hath no money; come ye, buy, and eat; yea, come, buy wine and milk without money and without price' (*Isa.* 55:1). Jesus Christ invites all those who labour and are heavy laden to come to him, and he will give them rest. God is honest in his invitations. Be sure of that. If God invites you, he wants you to accept the invitation. After reading the many invitations of the Word of God to you, you may not say, 'If I may.' It will be a wicked questioning of the sincerity of God.

In addition to being invited, you are entreated. Many passages of Scripture go far beyond a mere invitation. God persuades and entreats you to come to him. He seems to cry like someone who is weeping, 'As I live, says the Lord God, I have no pleasure in the death of the wicked; but that the wicked turn from his way and live: turn ye, turn ye . . . for why will ye die, O house of Israel?' (*Ezek.* 33:11). Our Lord and Master when he made the feast, and those who were asked did not come, sent out his servants to compel them to come in. He used more than a bare invitation, he put forth a divine compulsion. I would entreat, persuade, exhort all of you who have not believed in Jesus to do so now. In the name of Jesus, I beseech you to seek the Lord. I do not merely put it to you, 'Will you or will you not?' but I would lay my whole heart by the side of the request and say to you, 'Come to Jesus. Come and rest your guilty souls on him.' Do you not understand the gospel message? Do you know what it asks and what it gives? You shall receive perfect pardon in a moment if you believe in Jesus. You shall receive a life that will never die— receive it now, quick as a lightning flash, if only you trust in the Son of God. Whoever you may be, and whatever you may have done, if with your heart you will believe in him whom God has raised from the dead, and obey him thereafter as your Lord and Saviour, every kind of sin and iniquity shall be forgiven you. God will blot out your iniquities like a cloud. He will make you begin *de novo*—fresh, anew. He will make you a new creature in Christ Jesus. Old things shall pass away and all things become new.

But there is the point—believing in Jesus; and you may look me in the face and cry, 'But may I?' May you? Why, you are exhorted, invited, entreated to do so. Nor is this all. You are even commanded to do it. This is the commandment—that you believe on Jesus, whom he has sent. This is the gospel: 'He that believeth and is baptized shall be saved; but he that believeth not shall be damned' (*Mark* 16:16). There is a command, with a threatened punishment for disobedience. Shall anybody say, 'May I?' after that? If I read, 'Thou shalt love the Lord thy God with all thy heart', do I say, 'May I love God?' If I read, 'Honour thy father and thy mother', do I say, 'May I honour my father and my mother?' No. A command is a permit and something more. It gives full allowance and much more. As you will be damned if you do not believe, you have therefore been given a right to believe—not only a permission, but a warrant of the most practical kind. Oh, can you not see it? Will you not cry to God: 'Lord, if you will damn me if I do not believe, you have given me a full gospel liberty to believe. Therefore I come and put my trust in Jesus.' 'If I may'—I think that this questioning ought to come to an end now. Will you not give it up? May the Holy Spirit show you, poor sinner, that you may now lay your burden down at Jesus' feet, and be saved at once. You may believe. You have full permission now to confess your sin and to receive immediate pardon: see if it is not so. Cast your guilty soul on him, and rise forgiven and renewed, henceforth to live in fervent gratitude, a miracle of love.

14

A Needless Question Answered

'If I may be permitted to touch the hem of his garment, I shall be made whole.' But there arises this bitter question, 'BUT CAN I? I know that I may if I can; but I cannot.' Now that is the question I am going to answer. The will to believe in Christ is as much a work of grace as faith itself, and where the will is given and a strong desire, a measure of grace is already received, and with it the power to believe. Do you not know that the will to commit adultery is, according to Scripture, reckoned as adultery? He 'hath committed adultery with her already in his heart.' Now, if the very thought of uncleanness and the will towards it is the thing itself, then a desire or will to believe contains within itself the major part of faith. I do not say that it is all, but I do say this—that if the power of God has made a man will to believe, the greater work has been done, and his actually believing will follow in due course.

The entire willingness to believe is nine-tenths of believing. Inasmuch as to will is present with you, the power which you do not find as yet will certainly come to you. The man is dead, and the hardest thing is to make him live; but in the case before us the quickening is accomplished, for the man lives so far as to will: he wills to believe, he yearns to believe, he longs to believe; how much has been done for him! Rising from the dead is a greater thing than the performance of an act of life. Faith in Christ is the simplest action that anybody ever performs. It is the action of a child; indeed, it is the action of a new-born babe in grace. A new-born babe never performs an action that is very complicated. We say, 'Oh, it is such a babyish thing,' meaning that it is so small. Now faith comes at the moment that the child is born into God's family; it occurs at the same time as the new birth. One of the first signs and tokens of being born again is faith; therefore it must be a very, very simple thing. I venture to say that faith in Christ differs in no respect from faith in anybody else, except in the person upon whom that faith is set. You believe in your mother: you may in the same way believe in Jesus Christ, the Son of God. You believe in your friend: it is the same act that you have to do toward your higher and better Friend. You believe the news that is commonly reported and printed in the daily journals: it is the same act which believes Scripture and the promise of God.

The reason why faith in the Lord Jesus is a superior act to faith in anyone else lies in this fact—that it is a superior person whom you believe in, and superior news that you believe; and your natural heart is more averse to believe in Jesus than to believing in any one else. The Holy Spirit must teach your faith to grasp the high things of Christ Jesus; but that grasp is by the hand of a simple, childlike faith. But it is the same faith. It is the gift of God in so far as this—that God gives you the understanding and the judgment to exercise it upon his Son, and to receive him. The faith of a child in his father is almost always a wonderful faith, just the faith that we would ask for our Lord Jesus. Many children believe that there is no other man in the world so great and good, and right and kind, and rich and everything else, as their father is; and if anybody were to say that their father was not so wonderful, they would become quite grieved; for if their father is not a king, it is a mistake that he is not. Children think like this about their parents, and that is the kind of faith we would have you exercise towards the Lord Jesus Christ, who deserves such confidence, and much more. We should give to Jesus a faith by which we do him honour and magnify him greatly.

[83]

Just as the child never thinks where the bread and butter is to come from tomorrow, and it never enters its little head to fret about where it will get new socks when the present ones are worn out, so you must trust in Jesus Christ for everything you want between here and heaven—trust him without asking questions. He can and will provide. Just give yourself up to him entirely, as a child gives itself up to a parent's care, and feels itself to be at ease. Oh, what a simple act it is, this act of faith! I am sure that it must be a very simple act, and cannot require great wisdom because I notice that the wise people cannot do it; the strong people cannot do it; the people who are righteous in themselves cannot reach it. Faith is a kind of act which is performed by those who are childlike in heart, whom the world calls fools, and ridicules and persecutes for their folly. 'Not many wise men after the flesh, not many mighty, not many noble, are called: but God . . . hath chosen the weak things of the world . . . And base things . . . and things which are despised hath God chosen' (*1 Cor.* 1:26–27). There are people with no education whatever who just know their Bibles are true, and have an abundant faith: they are poor in this world, but rich in faith. Happy people! Alas, for those wise people whose wisdom prevents faith in Jesus! They have been to more than one university, and have earned all the degrees that carnal wisdom can bestow upon them, and yet they cannot believe in Jesus Christ, the Son of God. Oh, friend, do not think that faith is some difficult and puzzling thing, for then these senior wranglers and doctors of divinity would have it. It is the simplest act that the mind can perform.

'But shall I not have to do many good works?' says somebody. You shall do as many as you like when you are saved; but in this matter of your salvation you must fling all self-righteousness away as so much devilry that will ruin and injure you, and come simply to Christ, and Christ alone, and trust in him.

[84]

'Oh,' says another, 'I think I see a little light. If I am enabled—if I get enough power to trust in Jesus, I shall be made whole.' I will ask another question: Do you not know that *you are bound to believe in Christ*—that it is Christ's due that he be believed in? My own conviction is that a great many of you can, and that already, to a large extent, you do; only you are looking for signs and wonders which will never come. Why not exert that power a little farther? The Spirit of God has given to you a measure of faith; oh, believe more fully, more unreservedly. Why, you shiver at the very thought of doubting Christ. You felt how unjust and wrong it was; there is latent in you already a faith in him. 'He that believeth not God hath made him a liar' (*1 John* 5:10). Would you make Christ a liar? Why not bring faith to the front and say, 'I do believe, I will believe, that the Christ who is the Son of the Highest, and who died for the guilt of men, is able to save those who trust him, and therefore I trust him to save me. Sink or swim, I trust him. Lost or saved, I will trust him. Just as I am, with no other plea but that I am sure that he is able and willing to save, I cast my guilty soul on him'? You have the power to trust Jesus when you have already yielded to the conviction that he is worthy to be trusted. You have only to push to its practical conclusion what God the Holy Spirit has already wrought in you, and you will at once find peace.

Still, if you think that there is something that prevents your having faith in Christ, though you know that if you had it you would be saved, I earnestly entreat you not to stay contentedly for a single hour without a full, complete, and saving faith in Christ; for if you die as an unbeliever, you are lost, and lost forever. Your only safety lies in believing in the Lord Jesus Christ with all your heart, and obeying his commandments.

SOME OTHER

BANNER OF TRUTH

TITLES

RIGHT WITH GOD

John Blanchard

Right With God is a straightforward book to help those searching for a personal faith in God. It has been widely used throughout the English-speaking world and translated into many other languages.

'This book is a prize indeed. John Blanchard uses his considerable powers of analysis to set out the great truths of the gospel in a way that is both clear and compelling. Thank God for it!' *The Rev J. A. Motyer, one-time Principal of Trinity College, Bristol.*

'John Blanchard writes as clearly as he speaks, so that misunderstanding is impossible. I do not know any book quite like it.' *The Rev R. C. Lucas, St. Helen's, Bishopgate, London.*

'The best modern book we have seen for explaining the gospel to the serious non-Christian.' *Come.*

'Buy it, read it, and make use of it!' *The Evangelical Presbyterian.*

John Blanchard is an internationally-known evangelist and Bible Teacher. A co-founder of Christian Ministries, he is the author of many books and his other work includes radio and television broadcasting.

ISBN 0 85151 045 0
128pp. Paperback